Business Process Management with a Business Rules Approach

Business Process Management with a Business Rules Approach

Implementing the Service-Oriented Architecture

Tom Debevoise

Tipping Point Solutions, Inc.

Tipping Point Solutions, Inc.
Roanoke, Virginia 24019

Library of Congress Cataloging in Publication Data

These books are widely used by corporations and government agencies for training, marketing and resale. The publisher offers discounts on this book when ordered in bulk quantities.

For more information, contact Corporate Sales Department, Phone +1 (540) 314-3923 E-mail: tdebevoise@tipping-point.net

ISBN: 978-1-4196-7368-9

LCCN: 2005903977

Printed in the United States of America

To Barb

Table of Contents

FOREWORD

Can you imagine a business, government agency, or nonprofit organization that does not incorporate business processes into its operation? Every enterprise mission is defined by the processes' cyclical series of operations. Computer systems support many of these processes, and systems need accurate information to decide what to do. These decisions mediate the flow of information between the actors in the enterprise. In the steps of the business process, managers and information technology (IT) personnel refer to such mediators as business rules. Business rules specify how an entity will use information in its decision-making process. Because business rules trigger critical decisions, and an organization's mission is achieved through the use of business processes, both need to be thoughtfully captured and preserved. If it were possible, wouldn't it be worthwhile to preserve business processes and business rules with software?

Every large organization or enterprise maintains in-house computer applications that perform business processes and apply business rules to data. These applications connect systems, users, and their enterprise partners to ERP packages. The application is a critical part of the enterprise business process, yet it is difficult and expensive for the responsible teams to mold these applications around changes in processes and rules. This is because most applications are not created using a model of the business process. Most IT shops are also building applications using techniques or methods that predate Business Process Management (BPM) or business rules.

BPM and business rules methods and software are not just technical jargon or high-tech hype. BPM and business rules are modern ways for teams to model the business process, business rules, and Web services that serve the process. Today, there are plenty of available software packages that help to carry out BPM and business rules. Because most organizations manually manage their business processes, this software has business productivity benefits. It also improves an organization's productivity through business process reengineering.

With the IT budget of a commercial organization costing between 6-20 percent of its operating budget, one CIO magazine article estimates that 60 percent of this cost is for integration applications. I believe that BPM and business rules can dramatically cut the total cost of integration maintenance by cutting costs and providing productivity improvements. I want to show you how this reduction in the cost of integration can happen with the use of a new class of software: Business Process and Business Rules suites (BPM/BR).

The long-range benefit of this new approach occurs when an organization maintains its applications with an automated model of business processes and business rules. The savings are realized when an organization is able to smoothly adapt the business processes to its needs. BPM/BR suites ease that transition because the vendors have designed this software with the flexibility to update and modernize processes with much more efficient methods than in the past.

Will the cost of this new method be a good investment? Nicholas Carr explains the case that information technology has become a commodity for business in his controversial Harvard Business Review article "IT Doesn't Matter." In a study of 7,500 companies, those that spent the least on IT were among the top performers. This, and other analysis, led him to suggest that overspending is the greatest risk in the IT industry. One way to cut the risk of overspending is for IT organizations to coordinate applications with a business model of the organization. To change a business rule or business process, you would simply change the model. This calls for a new architecture, a new class of integrated development environments, and smarter, more agile organizations.

BPM/BR server tiers run in what the IT industry is calling the service-oriented architecture (SOA). BPM/BR provides this feature so your IT management team can easily change parts of the technical infrastructure with the least amount of disruption. This new approach uses separate servers for business processes and business rules. The SOA approach connects these by means of Web services or messaging. In this book, I am going to stress the Web services approach. The advantage to the Web services approach is that you can use it both internally and externally.

This book describes a strategy for combining Business Process Management and the business rules approach (BPM/BR). This is an approach that combines four interrelated trends in systems development: business rules, Business Process Management, Enterprise Integration (EI), and Business Intelligence (BI). Rather than give a laundry list of tasks and deliverables, I am going to recount a project that uses BPM/BR. I hope that this will be an entertaining way of showing how to use this technique in your organization. I have developed a trial case for a construction equipment rental agency, Sumter Rents. I believe it will be small enough to cover in a book, yet show enough complexities to parallel the challenges organizations face.

BOOK CONTENTS

I have divided this text into the following chapters:

Introduction. The introduction presents the case of Sumter Rents. This mature business holds many challenges that I have drawn from my professional experience and the company that I work for—Business Knowledge Architects. I will describe how the service-oriented economy and outsourcing trend increase the need for BPM. I will describe why we need a method that combines Business Process Management (BPM) and the business rules approach.

Chapter 2, Business Architecture. This chapter presents some of the challenges for the management at Sumter Rents. These challenges comprise conventional business rules and processes, and present-day problems such as outsourcing services from other sellers. It also includes the use of a maintenance management module from an Enterprise Resource Planning (ERP) package. In this first phase, our team selects the objectives and goals of the project. They also develop a business case to justify the project. Typical of a business case, the participants in this task will develop what we want to reach for and what we will avoid. I will briefly describe a project management approach. The aim of the chapter is a firm foundation for a successful project.

Chapter 3, Business Process Management. This chapter describes how analysts build and improve the business processes for Sumter Rents. They prepare diagrams in Business Process Modeling Notation (BPMN). The project team improves and certifies the diagrams in a workshop setting. The project plan's objectives include developing an equipment process and processing customer reservations. First, analysts develop core business processes. These high-level diagrams also detail how business rules apply the information. In this part of defining the business process, the analysts also develop the decision areas of the businesses rules analysis. The outcome of this step is business process diagrams.

Chapter 4, Business Rules. This chapter describes how the project team builds business rules for the Sumter Rents business processes. Earlier, the business process diagrams identified sets of business rules for equipment maintenance and the customer folio. In workshops and interviews, our team develops the details of the business rules. As they finish the rules, a scribe models them into the Business Rules Repository (BRR). Next, the systems administrators expose each business object as a Web service. Lastly, the analyst connects the business process diagrams to the business object with a collaboration object that interacts with the Web service. The outcome of this activity is a system that is ready for testing and confirmation.

Chapter 5, Business Intelligence. This chapter describes how the business processes and business rules activities of the Sumter Rents project create and maintain the data warehouse. The first purpose of the BI system is to estimate an ideal rental inventory that matches projected customer demand. The project also supports business activity monitoring. The business rules in the BRR affect the design of the data warehouse. Business processes provide new information about customer behavior and retail performance. Your BPM software includes internal process timing information that you distill into efficiency metrics. The outcome of this activity is a data warehouse that helps managers understand what is happening in Sumter Rents.

Chapter 6, IT Convergence. BPM offers a powerful way to manage your legacy systems. If you have many legacy systems and many systems administrators, then there is a good chance that much of what they do can be managed by BPM software. This is called IT convergence. This chapter describes how to convert your legacy processes to a BPM environment. I describe how to add controls, error reporting, and logging standards. This development effort is not extensive. The controls I suggest adding are the ones that your organization does manually. As you add support for legacy processes to BPM, you start to add more advanced business processes to your environment. BPM puts a great deal of control in the hands of managers. Chapter 7 also describes process management.

Chapter 7, Technical Architecture. In this chapter, I present the characteristics of a technical architecture for the service-oriented environment. In previous chapters, I described two side effects of the new service-oriented economy—companies competing for market share outsource inefficient activities to cut costs, and publish their products and services on the Internet. A team uses the BPM/BR method to design flexible business processes that manage this. The organization's architecture, however, must also be flexible. This chapter describes the mission of the different tiers of the technical-oriented architecture.

Chapter 8, Transition. This chapter briefly covers some of the considerations of putting the project into production. A quality assurance team should test all business processes against valid data to confirm or deny that the system properly performs the business rules and processes. To avoid production issues, the team should also load test the entire application. I will describe how a configuration management group works with a BMP approach and a Business Rules Repository (BRR). The goal of this chapter is the goal of the project—a new production system.

Chapter 9, Conclusion. To close the book, I predict the benefits achieved by an enterprise that creates an IT environment from a model of how the business works. I believe that this will change the economics of an organization. Business modeling is an improvement over other forms of software engineering. Because modeling a business is fundamentally different from modeling data or objects, however, IT teams are certain to face a certain culture shock.

Suggested Reading Patterns

This textbook has two central tracks. The first is a description of a project that uses BPM/BR to complete a project. The other is an exposition that presents technical details of what the organization needs to understand.

You do not need to read every chapter to gain some benefit from this book. If you are a manager considering the use of BPM and business rules, and want to get a feel for how it would benefit your organization, then read Chapters 1 through 5. After the introductory chapter, the chapters answer these questions:

- **Chapter 2, Business Architecture:** What are the business systems problems that need to be addressed? What is the justification for the projects? When are we going to do them?
- **Chapter 3, Business Process Management:** What are the basic business processes that will construct the project solutions? How are we going to incorporate business rule architecture?
- **Chapter 4, Business Rules:** How do we discern and extract the business rules for our application? How do we implement the business rules software?
- **Chapter 5, Business Intelligence:** How do we improve executive decisions? What are the metrics for the decisions? What

is the relationship between the business rule, business processes, and the data warehouse?

- **Chapter 6, IT Convergence:** How to we manage legacy systems in a business-processing environment? How do we move legacy systems into the environment? What are the benefits to centralized management?
- **Chapter 7, Transition:** How do we create and deploy the application? How do we create a safe and stable system?

For the division manager, Chapters 2, 3, and 6 describe how a significant portion of the IT infrastructure may be reengineered.

The BPM/BR is a new way of completing integration projects. I feel it is the only application development approach that addresses the key objective of enabling organizations to create comprehensive, industry-specific business processes while reducing the cost, complexity, and time of cross-application integration.

The BPM/BR approach moves application integration from a complex and expensive technical challenge into a simple way to build applications for the enterprise and its customers and partners. The approach provides an integrated process-control architecture that achieves real-time visibility into parts of the business process. Not only do the integrated business rules and process control tactics enable organizations to place business processes quickly, they also yield the flexibility to adapt processes in response to quickly changing operational dynamics.

The objective of this approach is to create a single point of *plug and play* at a high level. Organizations are not locked into the rigid architecture of an integration that they have painfully created. They have the freedom to choose services from other companies and change applications and technology. Through a business rules and integrated process-control strategy, organizations finally realize the strategic benefits of full and flexible application integration at dramatically reduced cost, complexity, and time-to-deployment. This is the true nature of the agile organization.

I hope that we have presented a good roadmap with this text. There are tools and machinery in this book that will help designers seeking to improve their work. The objective of BPM/BR methods is to provide teams with the ability to build and control new systems that live with changing, abstract business models.

For news about the book and author please visit:

www.TomDebevoise.com

THANKS

I want to thank all of the people that helped me with this project, including Buddy Towne, Warren Capps, Tim Clotworthy, George Sarris, and Cindy Shearer. I want to especially thank Jim Bromhal for his many suggestions.

In this second printing, I especially want to thank Larry Goldberg of Knowledge Partners International for his many suggestions, tireless help and advice.

REFERENCES

Carr, Nicolas G, 2003 "IT Doesn't Matter", Boston MA, Harvard Business Review.

CHAPTER 1: INTRODUCTION

Is your IT infrastructure ready to respond to economic slowdowns, globalization, and outsourcing trends? What role would you play if your company or government agency moved a division offshore, or privatized a facet of the operation? To help with the critical role of process management, leading software companies have released new types of software, especially solutions for Business Process Management (BPM) and Business Rules Approach (BR). A business process is a repeating cycle that reaches a business goal. Business rules mediate the information in the business process. BPM and BR software support business goals by managing and running business processes and business rules. This class of software simplifies changes. They help your organization become more competitive by allowing you to respond to opportunities by simply adapting your business to the new world. Your IT organization, however, must change its methods to use BPM or BR software. The biggest change is conceptual—your software designers will no longer describe what the *software* does, they will describe what the *business* does.

BPM is responsible for lowering the boundary between the brick walls of businesses and the networked global economy. Through BPM, the most competitive companies are forging a close relationship with their customers and suppliers. The enterprise application integration (EAI) industry calls closely related groups of business services a "composite application." The composite application combines the services of everyone's systems into a virtual application. To build a composite application, you need to be able to expose your system services. There are two important standards for performing this—the Web services description language (WSDL) and the Business Process Execution Language (BPEL). When you develop your composite application with these languages, you create a Service-Oriented Architecture (SOA). Your IT organization needs a combination of Business Process Management and Business Rules Approach (BPM/BR) to build the composite application in an SOA.

Sumter Rents, Inc. is a leading construction equipment rental firm in the southeast United States. This company provides short- and long-term rental of heavy or specialized construction equipment to small, mid-sized and Fortune 500 companies. Sumter also leases smaller machinery and specialized hand tools to the consumer.

1

The construction rental market is a growing and profitable part of Sumter's business. Since the slowdown in the economy began, construction firms have augmented their fleets with leases of varying terms. This strategy has allowed many construction firms to cut their capitalized costs. Smaller companies also use leasing of construction equipment as leverage to aim for larger projects and other opportunities that they might not otherwise chase. Because contractor rentals are the largest part of their revenue, Sumter Rents wants to expand their share of this market. In Europe, construction firms lease up to 80 percent of their heavy equipment. Sumter sees a parallel opportunity for growth potential in the American rental market.

Sumter Rents has over 30 years of experience in the field. They lease and service over 700 types of equipment, including a wide range of bulldozers, backhoes, compaction rollers, work platforms (cherry pickers), cranes, air compressors, generators, and paving equipment. Other types of equipment include mobile storage and pumping equipment. They also lease smaller equipment to the homeowner market, including Bobcats, tractors, and hand tools.

Sumter's IT department has recently converted their legacy accounting systems into SAP R3. Sumter also uses the SAP Plant Maintenance (SAP PM) application. SAP PM is a software solution that potentially covers all maintenance tasks for Sumter. SAP PM plans and tracks all maintenance for system availability, costs, materials, and personnel placement.

Sumter wants to create a closer relation with their customers by providing them with rental and related information services on the Internet. Sumter understands that a service-oriented architecture is a key competitive technology in the current economy. As we will see, there are several key areas where Sumter will benefit from this business approach.

SUMTER RENTS: NEW SERVICE ORIENTED OFFERINGS

In foraging for a deeper alliance with construction companies, Sumter imagines a Web services model that will connect the rental fleet with customers' project and bid planning. Sumter intends to offer special discounts to these "special partners." One of the keys is for Sumter to identify high volume customers and offer discounted pricing via Web services to these customers. In exchange for registering, special partners will get a spreadsheet with a .NET pricing page that they use for planning projects. The hope is that customers will rapidly negotiate corporate contract terms that will grow the contractors' businesses as well as Sumter's rental business.

Sumter has integrated SAP with an old-fashioned hub-and-spoke IT environment. Their previous development methods buried processes and rules in many COBOL (80's), PL*SQL (90's), and ASP (00's) applications. The old ways have also scattered integration programs across their technical architecture. The current IT team knows it will need to adapt quickly to process changes and will need a Web services model. The business will need custom business processes for the preferred partners. Sumter wants to be able to change processes and rules so it can publish its new offerings on the Internet. With processes and rules buried in the computer code, it is difficult for them to do this.

MEETING TODAY'S CHALLENGES

Sumter Rents plans to overcome the difficulties of changing processes and rules by using a combination of Business Process Management and business rules approach (BPM/BR). Sumter hopes to develop a useful environment for customers and managers that will be easy to modify as business needs change. Organizations do this with a combination of commercial software and BPM/BR.

BPM/BR organizes integration into two separate areas: an environment of software and server(s) that is responsible for business processes, and another environment that is responsible for business rules. This arrangement simplifies updates to new software releases. The chief benefit of this is that there is a *zero administration* capability, because processes and rules are positioned for change. Another benefit is that the BPM/BR changes an organization's methods because it needs radically fewer personnel and shorter project cycles.

Zero administration for items that are positioned for change does not mean that they should not be thoroughly tested. It does mean that the change is easier to make.

Business Process Management (BPM) Defined

A business process is a sequence of activities that carries out a complete business goal. For example, when a customer fills out an order form, you do not consider it complete until the interface program posts the order to the ERP. Business Process Management is the identification, understanding, and management of business processes that link with people and systems in and across organizations.

There are plenty of new software packages that use Business Process Management to create systems. Examples include Intalio, Tibco and WebMethods.

Business Rules Defined

A business rule is a mediator of information in computer systems for decision-makers such as managers, employees, and salespeople. Business rules decide with information. When you change the business rule, you change the decisions. A business rule can be a policy, a constraint, or a regulatory requirement. An example of a business rule would be to filter the information needed to decide whether to extend credit to a customer. There are new classes of software that can take a group of business rules and create an entire application.

The business rules approach is a new design technique for formalizing an enterprise's critical business rules in a language the manager and technologist understand. Business rules create an unambiguous statement of what a business does with information to decide a proposition. The formal specification becomes information for process and rules engines to run. The language should be legible by the application engines. The clauses of the language include terms, data, translations, procedures and processes. The outcome of this procedure is metadata that describes the steps of a given rule, and is evaluated by engines. The result is a tool that collects, analyzes and models business rules and produces applications that implement them. The technical approach described here offers a strategic first step in modernizing the method of creating connected, not interfaced, technology solutions.

Composing the Service-Oriented Architecture with BPM/BR

A Service-Oriented Architecture (SOA) is both a design approach to information technology and a basic business strategy. A *service* in SOA is a piece of a computer system packaged as a reusable ingredient for use in a business process. The .NET spreadsheet that Sumter plans to use is a good example of this. Business process management (BPM) is a good strategy for modeling the processes and identifying opportunities for competitive improvement in an enterprise. The SOA connects BPM to the customer or trading partner.

BPM visualizes the current business as an *information chain*. An information chain connects a step-by-step series of activities with data. Think of the information chain as a macro business process, and SOA as the links. The process of construction contractors bidding on projects and performing services is an example. Sumter aims to be a tighter part of the information chain by forging a closer relationship with the contractors. As the value of a particular service of the business becomes clearer, managers outsource or cut out services. The business offers its special services and products to customers.

SERVICE-ORIENTED BUSINESSES NEED A COMPOSITE METHOD

If you are working with business systems such as the one we described for Sumter, then consider the new methods offered by BPM/BR. I believe that today these techniques should be an important part of your delivery methods. This chapter will show you how BPM/BR has worked, and how it will work for you.

MY EXPERIENCE WITH CHANGING METHODOLOGY

As an engineer with more than twenty years of experience, I develop ways of connecting business needs with technological capacities. I've developed:

- Computer applications for environmental modeling, automated data collection and supervisory control and data acquisition (SCADA) systems
- Diagnostics programs using expert systems, an artificial intelligence technique that analyzed a user's questions and provided probable solutions
- Maintenance management databases for public infrastructures— water, sewer and storm water systems—that selected what to do based on the different conditions of pipes, pumps, valves and other parts
- An enterprise clinical trial system, a cross-trial system that generated case report forms and stored data for the FDA's multiphase process
- Inventory management—specifically downstream integration—for the petroleum industry

I've had different roles in these projects, including developer, designer, systems administrator, and manager. In these roles, I've met many different types of organizational needs, and different design approaches to data and information processing. I've always been a part of organizations that solved problems by designing and programming computer applications.

My early career in 'hard engineering' taught me the value of rigorous design methods

Because application development is complex and challenging work, I have always sought to use the best design techniques for finishing my projects. My background in *hard* engineering taught me that doing a project with a disciplined design method must be a core value in my work.

Experience has taught me that creative project teams adapt current tools and methods to the needs of the project. For instance, some organizations have a greater need for explaining and agreeing to written requirements than others. Other projects need fewer group workshops because hardware interface controls drive the needs of that project, and there is little human involvement.

BPM/BR DESCRIBES THE BUSINESS, NOT THE TECHNICAL DETAILS

Business processes and business rules describe the business, not the technical details. I will show how these new design methods meet Sumter's challenges. I will also show how they work together to make it simple for an organization to update rules or processes without complicated redeployments of production systems.

BPM/BR represents a change in the language and symbols that we use to describe information systems—these methods have become more business-centered and less tied to the technical details of systems. In the past, the IT industry has moved first from information engineering (IE), to object-oriented software engineering (OOSE), to *use case* analysis. Along the way, commercial off-the-shelf (COTS) software became an important part of commonly used technology. The latest methods changed the focus from mathematical theories of data and functions into pictures and English sentences of what the business does. For instance, IE uses an entity relationship diagram (ERD). The ERD depicts relational calculus formulas. A business process diagram looks and acts like a white board, and business rules have written descriptions.

In the late 1980s and early 1990s, my practice focused on relational databases, and I did much of the design work with data modeling. James Martin's IE, (a data-centered approach) soon became a prevalent practice, and it spread throughout the IT industry. Some believed there were innate weaknesses in a *data-centric* approach. Because they might not record all process details, data models are incomplete artifacts. Data model needs programs to create records in the database. As the database changes, the programs that feed the database need to change as well. Next, OOSE arose to compete with IE. Both of these old methods have many champions to this day, yet neither of them connects business rules and business processes to the organization's applications.

By the late 1990s I was working with focused, solution-oriented software including business intelligence (BI), supply chain management (SCM), and customer relationship management (CRM). Every project that I work with increasingly involves integrating large systems COTS software. These customers develop and maintain fewer of their own applications by setting up COTS packages. They are making these changes because:

- Developing equivalent systems in-house is too expensive
- Commercial software improves the quality of the environment
- Commercial software carries out competitive commercial practices

Each need for integration involves business rules and business processes. With IE or OOSE, the developers bury rules and processes into their computer programs.

Data modeling and use case analysis create a technical snapshot of how the organization does business today. Businesses always need to change their processes and rules to remain competitive. Data modeling and use case analysis do not easily help with these changes in applications. So, in some ways, BPM/BR software is the next step in modern software. Instead of writing programs in Java or C, BPM/BR organizations model what the business does in words and diagrams. To update the process or rule, you update the diagrams and words.

In many industries—telecommunications, finance, healthcare—almost every process has already set up a data model. What these industries want to do is improve through cutting the cost of implementing new practices. They have begun to see the need for modeling the processes and the rules that feed their COTS packages, and they are using SOA to offer these processes to customers as a service.

PEOPLE AND ORGANIZATIONS NEED TO CHANGE

SOA presents a big challenge to the mature IT organization. The practice of software design has shifted its focus many times during the last 20 years, and the teams doing the work have a hard time following the trends. The exploding powers of software and hardware capacities have also contributed to this phenomenon. Organizations have struggled to keep up with advances in modern technology, and it will be a struggle for them to move to an SOA.

In my career, I have often witnessed poor management choices with technology. For instance, in the mid 1990s at a Telco, I met a team of at least 18 developers working to build their own database, even though most organizations had long since moved to commercial databases. The database development team situation may seem outrageous. But, even today, I meet teams that develop portals, process managers, and workflow solutions ... from *scratch*.

As a result, I have found that new application development methods need to be coupled with changes in the IT groups. Supporters of the new methods face a tough challenge: how to insert new ways of building applications into organizations that think the older ways of doing business are still valuable or successful.

I've decided that computing technology develops much faster than humans! What I've noted is that, while it is possible for a software package to offer a better, faster, and cheaper way of developing an application, it is very difficult for a group of people in an organization to change their ways to take advantage of it.

Even when organizations know of better ways to meet their IT challenges, it is difficult for them to change course and adopt them. I have heard managers compare their team's performance to a battleship's turning radius. They say that takes a long time to turn things around and change direction when information technology and business are moving in one direction. Even so, you have to wonder how groups that are in charge of mission-critical systems will use BPM, SOA, and business rules.

In the 1980s and 1990s, software engineering provided methods and tools for simplifying development, configuration, and testing. These development environments aided in the creation of screens, databases, and reports. You probably know that poorly used client-server tools, such as Sybase's PowerBuilder or Borland's Delphi, often put too many business rules in the client-side programs. In these tools, programmers put business rules code in the programs that ran the screens and reports. Hundreds or thousands of personal computers run these programs. On each computer is a version of the application and *run-time* software. A change to the business rules in the application code calls for expensive and painful redeployments of the client-server application. To change a business rule, the IT group has to redeploy the updated program to all client computers.

Web technology did not solve the problem of changes to client-server business rules. If programmers did not properly develop a Web application, then they did not position the business rules for simple changes. SOA moves the entire industry a step closer to an agile business.

ORGANIZATIONS NEED AN AGILE ARCHITECTURE: SOA

Because their current IT systems do not meet the objectives of executive management, their expectations can be ahead of the organization's abilities and behind the curve with the best competitive strategies. Management can take the following steps to improve the alignment:

- Adopting business process approaches to improve operations
- Offering portions of the business process to customers and trading partners
- Adopting commercial software packages

- Replacing or changing the legacy systems and processes; exposing the abilities of the systems to in-house systems and customers

Many organizations are striving to coordinate their business needs and their IT environments. Many enterprises are using BI and data warehousing to improve analytical decision-making and reporting requirements. They use commercial software for CRM, SCM, ERP, and other areas. The risk is that organizations may have poorly added BI, CRM, SCM or ERP into their system.

As businesses replace outdated or noncompetitive systems, they move processes and rules from the old systems into the integration programs. Executive management wants to improve the processes and rules. The problem is that the further back you go in time, the more difficult it is to change those processes or rules. This is because either the old design documentation is cryptic and incomplete, or someone must read and understand mysterious computer programs written in COBOL or C.

Because executive management expects systems to be able to adapt tactical changes in processes and rules, the way your organization adds COTS software to the system is an important choice. For this technical choice to be effective, you need to decide how to make technical systems work seamlessly with your business objectives. You need a virtual blueprint that effectively combines strategies and methods that handle changes in business rules and processes. The scheme should also preserve your investment in the best software and systems.

An adaptable solution—one that would be more agile—would be a combination of BPM software such as Tibco or Intalio, and business rules software such as Fair Isaac or Corticon. This combination builds an agile architecture—one that easily allows changes.

Web Services' Role In The Agile Architecture

The emerging power of Web services is a key to agile architectures. Web services are agile because you change them without changing the client programs. The Web services model is an effective architecture for the system that handles an enterprise. Web services are flexible because they integrate with a program as a client application, or they act as a server for many clients. This means that a Web service acts like a mini Web-server for your integration programs. For example, there are Web services that confirm European addresses. You could use the service in a program that validates an address before printing a shipping label. Client applications use these with a minimum amount of programming.

A Web service is a software system designed to support interoperable machine-to-machine interaction over a network. Web services employ industry standards so that they are compatible with many types of programming languages. XML documents describe Web services in a format known as Web services description language (WSDL). This is a new idea because a WSDL describes how a system takes advantage of the solutions that are on the Internet or intranet.

Web services promise to create systems that are open and adaptable. IT teams solve problems such as creating new business rules, processes, or interfaces. Once you solve these problems, you publish the solution to other applications as a WSDL. The Web service is visible inside the enterprise, or outside to the Internet. You might reuse the solution in other applications without rewriting the code. Because WSDL is a standard, it is easy to understand how to use the service.

Business Process Execution Language (BPEL) and the Composite Application

Business Process Execution Language (BPEL) extends Web services in an important way. BPEL orchestrates a collection of WSDLs. For example, the WSDLs involved in setting up contracts with a trading partner may involve activities such as "validate contract info" and "bid on contract" integrated with vendors' downstream legacy systems. In the Web services architecture, each of the WSDLs has specific inputs and outputs, and BPEL composes them. This is important because without an underlying orchestration, individual Web services are just individual instruments.

BPEL exposes services and powers that developers previously buried in systems. Without BPEL, the IT team must develop complicated interfaces that use hidden services and capacities. BPEL strengthens Web services and allows them to work with one another. BPEL orchestration also manages business processes. BPEL specifies steps that the business process automatically performs. The benefit of this is that BPEL:

- Removes complex interfaces
- Improves, changes, or cuts out unnecessary steps
- Reuses functionality with powers that BPEL publishes in the WSDL
- Makes costly code reengineering unnecessary
- Outsources business processes
- Offers portions of the process as a service to other customers

Composite applications are orchestrations of different programs and systems that act as one application. You use BPEL to create the composite application. Next, I am going to describe the role of business processes and business rules in the composite application.

Transition to the Way Forward

There are many benefits to building a composite application in an SOA. If you do it right, you can be competitive, and customers and trading partners will want to do business with you. I have found that this new environment is more agile and less costly to build and maintain. What you need is a method for getting there. My suggestion is to use a composite method—one that combines BPM and business rules.

PROCESS FOR A COMPOSITE METHOD

Creating and running the IT environment is a process. In the spirit of BPM, we consider a process that uses BPM and business rules to do this differently from IE or OOSE. The difference is that you view systems, such as ERP, as a provider of services. With BPM/BR, you define how your business uses the services.

The BPM/BR is a method that combines business rules, business process management, and architectural approaches. Collectively, these bring business rules, business processes, and other IT parts together in one step. In the same spirit, the BPM/BR encourages businesses to use COTS software.

Figure 1.1 presents a business process diagram of the BPM/BR. This figure introduces the business process model idea. A business process is an orchestration of activities that completes an important goal or purpose. This process diagram outlines the BPM/BR method. The diagram depicts the activities with labeled boxes. If the box has small squares in it, then the diagram hides details beneath the process. Because they are high level, I have collapsed the activities, but I will expand most activities in the coming chapters. The arrows show the flow from activity to activity. The circle depicts the state of the process with a starting activity and an ending state. At the top of the vertical *swim lanes*, the diagram labels the groups responsible for the various activities. The diagram shows decisions as diamonds, or pointy boxes. Parallel activities process concurrently. They branch from the horizontal lines that flow to the activities they spawn.

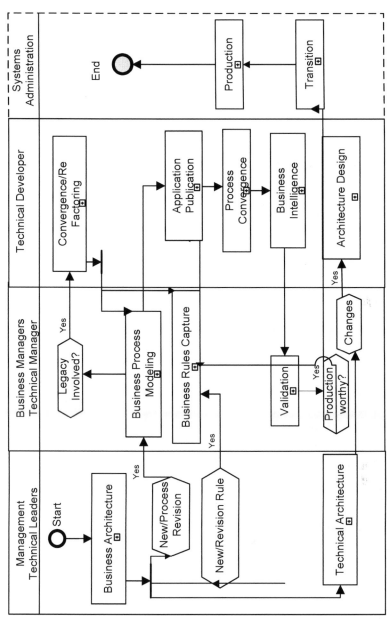

Figure 1.1 This business process diagram depicts the twelve basic activities in the BPM/BR.

With the process activities shown in Figure 1.1, the BPM/BR team creates the models for a solution that either carries out or updates a business process. The business processes and business rules create user interfaces, business-to-business (B2B) integration, COTS integration, and data warehouse ingredients. The metadata that describes these become important artifacts of the BPM/BR approach.

The BPM/BR approach creates data-driven specifications of an application's work. The business rules approach stores business rules as data in a database (metadata). BPM stores business processes as Business Process Modeling Notation (BPMN) in the BPM repository. BPMN also:

- Chooses and sequences activities
- Handles system errors or exceptions
- Handles process errors through compensations

For instance, a business process for a loan approval system might need to outsource employment verification to an external firm. An organization that uses BPM changes the process for handling this by changing the business process diagram.

The BPM/BR approach also preserves investments in older systems that they wish to keep by exposing their services on the Web. BPMN is independent of the language or system that provides service to a process. So it easily uses the legacy application as an activity.

There are many benefits to storing business rules as metadata in a business rules repository (BRR). Because a BRR works through sentences and data, you easily change the language to produce a needed product. Because the sentences in the BRR are simple to read, nontechnical managers are able to update them. For instance, a contracting organization might have policies allowing a customer to order an item from several different trading partner contracts. In another contracting scenario, there could be rules for payment of different transport types—based on the final destination. Business rules and processes are simple to create and update when the business expresses their processes in BPMN, and their policies in English words. BPMN software creates BPEL to run the process, and the phrases of business rules run the steps that enforce them. In the example, the business user changes the sentence that specifies some orders assigned to a contract, or they add a new transport mechanism. The result is that it is faster to update the responsible applications.

Throughout a BPM/BR process cycle, project managers need to oversee how well the team carries out the objectives, the extent of progress, and how efficiently the organization finishes cycles. Project managers need to direct and measure the efforts of a team with specific roles and responsibilities.

Now I want to describe the highlights of the activities shown in Figure 1.1. Because business process repositories and business rules repositories are recent technologies, the outcome of the activities feeds into the others in a new way. There is a new type of output in each of the activities: business processes, business rules, business intelligence, and technical architecture.

BPM/BR Process Activities

Of the basic activities in Figure 1.1, the five critical activities are:

- *Business Architecture:* The management team addresses the strategic and tactical goals of the business in a way that leverages the new world of business processes. The activity has steps for identifying services that the business should publish or use in their composite application. The outcome of the business architecture is a portfolio of projects.

- *Business Process Modeling:* For each project that improves the business architecture, the technical/management team creates a prototype of a business process model. To do this, the team first builds a high-level visual model in BPMN. BPMN looks a bit like the diagrams that people draw on white boards—a collection of boxes and arrows. Each box represents an activity, and the lines and arrows represent the streams of information between them.

- *Business Rules Capture:* The business rules approach specifies the business process validation needs in a precise language. Through discovery processes, such as workshop sessions, the language incrementally builds business rules. The aim is to foster a method that simplifies the maintenance of the application.

- *Business Intelligence:* BI is a natural outcome of the BPM/BR method. You compose a data warehouse from the business rules, processes, and transactions in the business process. Much of the information needed for a data schema for the data warehouse arises from information you gathered in previous steps. Often you need to support a statistical decision model, and this will guide you. There are, however, intrinsic data warehouse powers in every transactional system.

- *Technical Architecture:* The aim of BPM is to break down the barriers between IT and business. If this is your goal, you will need to modernize your technical architecture and simplify its administration. The types of software I am describing improve the connection between business tactics and applications.

In summary, the BPM/BR orchestrates business and IT. By orchestrate, I mean the systems do what the business needs them to do, not what legacy systems developers created it to do. This method provides business managers with the information technology they need. The BPM/BR approach combines business rules and BPM into a unified approach. I will describe how these new tools improve the construction of the operational system, data warehousing, and the integration process. The result is a powerful system that saves the organization time and money by allowing it to run the system with a smaller, more skilled staff, and shorter development cycles.

The BPM/BR modernizes the way we build today's business information architectures. It replaces outmoded ways of developing the IT environment. Before, IT would cobble together competitive, once leading-edge technologies in the IT ecosystem with hardwired methods. These retrofits resulted in a rigid technical architecture. The BPM/BR overcomes this by addressing integration, BI, and systems in one process. It avoids retrofitting the environment by creating loosely coupled business processes that simply add new solutions, COTS, or analytical tools.

SUCCESS WITH BPM/BR

In 2000, the Department of Defense faced a challenge. It rapidly needed to deploy an inventory management system to almost 90 wholesale fuel distribution centers around the world. These centers had low numbers of transactions each month (fewer than 50). The Defense Logistics Agency (DLA) management faced the potential cost of deploying an aging, thick client application at a cost of over $2.7M. Business Knowledge Architects was responsible for the integration server. We'd used a business rules approach to developing interfaces and the data warehouse, and were able to use the techniques described in this book to create a Web application.

In fewer than 60 days, the application was quickly tested and put into production. The implementation has been a success and has been deployed to over 150 locations worldwide, saving the DOD over $4M.

SUMMARY

- Competitive businesses are forging closer alliances with their customers and trading partners. An important way to do this is to expose their offerings on the Internet.

- To remain competitive, businesses must rapidly adapt their business processes and business rules.
- A business rule is a mediator of a business decision.
- A business process is a sequence of activities that achieves a goal.
- Enterprise architecture has changed over the last decade. There is more use of COTS and data warehouses. One of the most expensive line items in an Enterprise IT budget is integration. It is expensive to combine these elements.
- Old design methods are steeped in mathematical terminology that only a few understood. The methods of BPM/BR improve the way technical teams design business systems by describing what the business does, not what the computer systems do.
- BPM and the SOA is not only a technical innovation, it is a business strategy. BPM and SOA will be a critical part of the outsourcing revolution.
- Web services are a critical part of the SSO.
- The BPM/BR method is a process for developing systems that integrate their systems internally and externally. The process also exposes a business's services on the Internet.

REFERENCES

Smith H, and Fingar P (2003) *Business Process Management* Meghan-Kiffer Press: Tampa, Florida

von Halle B (2002) *Business Rules Applied,* John Wiley & Sons: New York

CHAPTER TWO: BUSINESS ARCHITECTURE

How do you begin to realize the vision of the SOA, with all the IT refuse of the past 20+ years around you? I suggest you spend some time thinking about what your enterprise should look like in a BPM world. I call this step the *business architecture*, and during this phase, projects are planned for connecting your business into the networked, service-oriented economy.

Previously, businesses produced products from the ground up—companies created parts, assembled them, sent them to market, and then sold them directly to customers. This model is rapidly disappearing. Most large industries have outsourced everything from parts manufacturing to customer financing. In the Harvard Business Review article entitled "Will You Survive the Outsourcing Revolution?" Uday Karmarkar argues that competitive businesses exist because of their position in an information chain. The information chain is a network of services for transactions and queries searching for the most efficient use of capitol in the economy. To take part, a company, individual, or government must expose and incorporate their services into many composite applications. In other words, your customers should incorporate your special offerings into their processes. To me, this sounds like the old academic axiom: *publish or perish.* Your potential customers will go elsewhere if they don't know that you have the services that they need. BPM is the emerging method for publishing and outsourcing a business's services and connecting these with others.

The business case that we are studying is a good example of how outsourcing affects business tactics. First, businesses lease equipment because they need short-term resources. To cut their capitalized costs, construction companies now lease a portion or part of their fleet. Construction businesses can be more competitive when they augment their fleet with leases. In another example, Sumter Rents is selling their fleet maintenance capacities to third-party organizations.

Sumter has 70 leasing outlets throughout the South, with some operations in the Midwest. With the rise in the rental industry, they have experienced rapid growth, and in the last fiscal year they turned over $220M in revenue.

Through years of maintaining a large fleet of equipment, Sumter has developed a skilled maintenance department. Their reputation in this area is so great that some manufacturers have outsourced their service care to them. Sumter's customers have also begun to outsource the care and maintenance of their fleets of equipment.

Sumter's growth has come at a cost. Sumter has bought 20 smaller rental firms, and integrating these companies has not been easy. The new maintenance staff is skilled, yet their practices are inconsistent. Sumter prides itself on being able to do business with a wide range of customers, yet the regional offices often have a problem balancing inventory and sharing equipment. When stores do not share equipment, the company disappoints customers and loses revenue. In addition, the customer service team has not efficiently scheduled and delivered equipment to customers.

As I wrote in the Introduction, Sumter Rents uses SAP's Plant Maintenance module (SAP PM) as an automated fleet maintenance solution. SAP PM has had benefits, yet there have been miscues in work orders. Because usage hours (how many hours on the odometer) drives the maintenance schedules of most heavy equipment, data entry errors might cause SAP PM to produce mistaken work orders. Not every Sumter retail branch is properly using the powers of SAP PM. The current process needs much manual effort. They need a simpler process.

Sumter has a good Web presence for their customers. Customers can view their account information, including accounts receivable and the equipment that they have rented out. They can't, however, order equipment or see when the equipment that they need will become available. Customers have asked that the Web be able to alert them when named types of equipment are available. Increasingly, customers want to seek certified operators with their equipment. Using its relationship with several labor contractors, Sumter hopes to increase its services by allowing customers to order labor.

As the CEO of Sumter, David's goal is to build his business from fourth place to third place in the Southeast. He aims to do this by improving the customer's rental experience. He has developed a three-step plan of action:

- Become the commercial customer's best partner in the rental industry through an extended partnership, from project planning to operator staffing and efficient delivery
- Become the premier source for equipment fleet maintenance. Offer a comprehensive plan for fleet maintenance using the SAP PM system

SUMTER'S BUSINESS OBJECTIVES AND STRATEGY

The CEO of Sumter is David Edmond Burk III. David is the grandson of the founder and majority shareholder.

- Keep an inventory of the most modern fleet of equipment available, by accurately assessing the need for new rentals and by timely selling of their existing fleet at the best price

David is a visionary in his field, and he grasps the complexities of what he wants his team to do. In some of his meetings he describes an ideal environment with all problems solved. Some of his visions have included:

- Provide model service for all lease orders. Incorporate the customer's reasoning in the order details, bid orders, and equipment mobilization. Create a single, predictable fee for mobilizing equipment
- Use radio frequency identification (RFID) to verify the equipment's run hours; download the information from the engine information module
- Plan efficient transportation and mobilization of all equipment flatbeds so that they roll from store to customers with the fullest possible loads
- Create a model of when to sell equipment, and take advantage of offshore variation in prices while balancing rental income from depreciated equipment

David wants to improve the balance of instore inventory and the business process of reselling used equipment. Rapidly rising prices in China and other areas create the opportunity to rotate out older equipment. This economic analysis would better match the company's inventory with sales demands and improve the age of the overall Sumter fleet. Sumter Rents might dispose of equipment at a profit; however, they must balance the numbers against the rental income, cost of sales, and the service to the customer. The current system is not rigorous enough to adequately handle such calculations, and is largely based on out-of-date information and many managers' guesses. Dave thinks these areas should be more carefully analyzed.

Sumter's Business Challenges

Successful leaders focus on opportunities. Business challenges, therefore, should first address opportunities, then problems. I frame a business challenge as a circumstance or question, which—supplied with effort, information, people, or capital—results in a capitalized opportunity. Secondly, a business challenge is a circumstance or question that might result in a solved problem. These are Sumter Rents top business challenges:

- Sales and customer service are improved with more information from the existing customer portal
- Sumter Rents needs to develop a closer partnership with its largest customers
- Sumter Rents aims to develop a revenue source by servicing customer-owned equipment

When the equipment a customer needs is unavailable, he will often look elsewhere. To offset this tendency, Sumter could notify customers when the equipment they need becomes available. Some customers even want this announcement sent to their mobile computers. Sumter Rents hopes to give this information in a timely and interactive way.

When customers use the portal, Sumter also could suggest productivity improvements that are targeted at, and useful to, the customers. The payoff for Sumter Rents is that it improves its rental income by providing companion rental equipment and services for the customer's job. Suggestions may include:

- Scheduling equipment operators from labor trading partners
- Building small business cases for more expensive, yet more efficient, rental selections

Sumter Rents' biggest challenge is gaining a closer partnership with its best customers—the large construction firms. These companies lease equipment for longer periods and significantly lengthen the lease periods. This improves the profitability of rental units. Sumter intends to use its services and information systems to tighten its partnership with these businesses. The customer, therefore, should be able to plan for a project—even months in advance—when he is preparing a project bid. In a traditional Web model, a contractor might download a price list and copy the data into a spreadsheet. Next, the contractor prepares his bid including material, labor mobilization, site preparation, and equipment.

What the new service-oriented model suggests is that this price list should be loaded into the spreadsheet as a .NET component. In fact, Sumter has been pondering a new *rental process* spreadsheet that would combine the price list, notices of needed equipment, and suggested equipment rental strategies.

A .NET component is an Internet service that customers access from a variety of manners including Web browsers and spreadsheets. BPM and Business Rules software enables the publication of these Web services. By publishing the Web service, your customers and trading partners easily incorporate them into your Internet services. This is known as *exposing* the Web service to the public.

Another challenge facing Sumter is how to cut the cost of coordinating equipment delivery. When equipment is not available locally, it is sent from the nearest location. A clerical team prints out all the delivery orders for the current week and posts them on a magnetic board. They visually inspect the board for bottlenecks and try to remove them. This process creates volatile delivery costs. Because the process is prone to errors, Sumter's management wants an automated solution.

The CEO wants to expand contract maintenance of contractor-owned equipment. A services-oriented system would expand the maintenance offerings to other organizations. The powers of SAP PM could be exposed as another Web service. When a contractor subscribes to the service, he could use another .NET or Web service application to post the utilization hours to Sumter's SAP PM system, and the business process could push the maintenance repair orders. The SAP PM Web service should first be built for internal use so that it meets the needs of the regional offices. Sumter personnel include trained maintenance crews, yet they are not getting all the work orders.

Sumter's Business Strategy and the SOA

Sumter's business strategy is a good example of the use of an economic sector's composite information chain. In the construction industry, this chain flows from project design to competitive bidding to contract award to construction and finally to inspection. Sumter connects to the chain with data for bidding and equipment and labor for construction.

The SOA is a combination of technology and design approaches that allow a company to combine their business processes with customers and vendors in the economy. The strategy has two core strengths: the lower cost of equipment, and the ability to maintain that equipment. OEM partnerships allow Sumter to buy the equipment in bulk at a lower price. Their maintenance skills allow them to offer leases at a lower price. They again lower the cost by selling the used equipment to near and offshore sources. Contractors' capital should naturally seek this efficiency. Because Sumter publishes these services on the Internet, their business process positions these strengths in the construction industry.

A PROCESS FOR DEVELOPING BUSINESS ARCHITECTURE

Figure 2.1 presents a business process for the business architecture activity of the BPM/BR method. The process first develops a business model and continues to develop business cases for projects that align the need gaps of the enterprise.

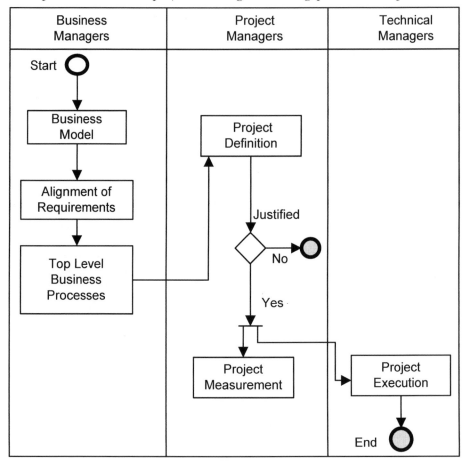

Figure 2.1 A business process for business architecture develops a project portfolio that aligns business strategy gaps with projects.

Concept Diagram for Business Architecture

Figure 2.2 presents a diagram of the concepts of the business architecture process. Figure 2.2 is not a data model; it outlines the topics, software, output, and information flowing through the activities of the business architecture process. The idea shows how the alignment activity creates candidates for BPM projects. The staff should justify each project candidate with a business case, priority, scope definition, and time frame. Several projects may affect several business processes. After the process, the technical team does the selected projects in the following processes of the BPM.

Figure 2.2 The business process for business architecture utilizes this concept schema to perform its work.

A business model is carried out by business processes. Business processes are governed by business policies that should be enforced by business rules. A performance gap or strategy/capability alignment problem should be corrected with new or adjusted processes and policies.

After most business processes, I am going to present a concept diagram. These diagrams will logically describe the types of data that activities use in the preceding process diagram. Through this approach I hope to avoid the technical tedium of entity relationship diagrams or object hierarchies. A capable data modeler should be able to convert a concept diagram into a data model.

SUMTER'S BUSINESS ARCHITECTURE

Obviously, I can not present every aspect of Sumter Rent's business architecture. Consider the challenges that this company faces. Sumter executive management plans to tackle the CEO's strategic goals for the business in a way that will meet these objectives:

- Expand the customer's online self-service options: accept reservations, add corporate discounts, tell customers of available equipment
- Reduce maintenance costs by improving the business process of using SAP PM, position the business process as a customer service
- Offer equipment operators from a trading partner to customers
- Balance inventory against projected demand and resell the aging inventory at the ideal time and price

Because they want collaboration with customers and trading partners, these objectives are only practical with a composite application. We will need BI for the last requirement. When we tackle these goals, we'll see that Sumter's executive management will need to direct the strategies and objectives within the contexts of the business. Because IT plays such a big role, the technical team's project cycles provide systems integration for this vision.

Sumter executives have appointed an IT management team that has the authority to initiate, monitor, and control the projects that are decided. The activities of business architecture become the first step for improving and modernizing the business infrastructure.

Aligning Business Strategies with Systems in a Service-Oriented Approach

Sumter Rents' business model aims to align the parts of their existing process model to meet the goals and challenges that I have discussed. Success will give Sumter Rents the most competitive business practices in the rental industry. The practice has changed from the customer-service model for the equipment rental business. First, there has been consolidation of small equipment rental companies.

This consolidation has lowered prices and increased the variety of offerings. Next, the Internet service model simplified shopping for equipment. Now, businesses expectations in a service-oriented economy and the Internet also change the competitive model. The .NET *rental process* worksheet I described is a competitive practice. Another competitive practice is combining SAP PM software power with Sumter's maintenance abilities.

The BPM movement is already changing many of Sumter Rent's commercial practices. For instance, BPM has affected Sumter Rent's relations with customers in the areas of retail and finance. Sumter's trading partners include manufacturing, service industries, insurance, and increasingly, Sumter utilizes services that are offered on the Internet. For instance, Sumter sees their supplier's order delivery schedule through the Internet. Sumter Rents has outsourced customers' credit references to other companies. Sumter uses a number of products that have off-shored customer support.

As well as specific vertical business practices, consider the universal practices of accounting, logistics, planning, economic data gathering, and human resources. My point is that any special competence or competitive advantage can be exposed as a service for others to use. We see this in Sumter Rents' plan to combine equipment and labor into one resource. Sumter's hope is that their competitive advantage will grow along with their expanded service offerings.

Because Sumter's management has decided to evaluate new business processes in maintenance, and especially a new product line in contract maintenance, the managers should perform a *gap* analysis. In the gap analysis, the Sumter IT management team decides the needs of the organization and then evaluates these against the current IT environment. The purpose is to evaluate, qualify, and quantify the difference between the systems they have and the ones they need. The Sumter IT management team inventories the building blocks of the organization's activities and then contrasts that set of activities with the current IT environment. For example, Sumter wants to replace their manual scheduling system, therefore Sumter's management will need to evaluate logistical software.

Sumter's Basic Business Model

Business architectures classify the types of core interactions that manage the units of work of the organization, including buy-side types (such as ordering, replenishment), and sell-side types (such as offerings, contracting, salvage). There may be others, such as taxes or financial transactions. For Sumter, the classifications are:

- Buy Side—buy equipment, order spare parts, and pass-through labor

- Sell Side—customer equipment leases, customer labor, used equipment sales

Next, the management team develops a simple, top-level diagram of Sumter's business process. They then map it to the supporting systems. The purpose of this mapping is to develop project plans. At this early stage, Sumter management needs to decide if the business needs to replace one more of the legacy practices or systems with commercial software. If not, the technical team should build interfaces to the legacy system, publish them as Web services, and control them with business processes. .

Sumter is going to phase their old maintenance management process into a part of a composite application. Here, the integration software will *gate* the processes to the legacy system. Gating a system in a composite application allows the old systems to be gradually phased out. This phase out could occur by division or geographic region. This strategy coordinates commercial software applications with the business operations and enterprise architecture. We hope it also reduces any concerns the organization might have about the cost of integrationFigure 2.3 presents the core activities for the CEO's goal of expanding Sumter Rents into the top three marketplace leaders by developing a closer relationship with key customers. The project areas are summarized in Table 2.1.

Figure 2.3 This diagram depicts Sumter's core activities. The project portfolio is developed from these activities.

Table 2.1 The business areas and the alignments needed to meet the aims of Sumter Management.

Business Area	Support System	Needed Alignment
Equipment Purchases	SAP Inventory	Business intelligence
Order provisioning	Manual Scheduling	Comprehensive Automated Logistics
Equipment maintenance	SAP PM	Composite Web application, service for posting equipment usage hours
Customer Leases	Sumter Customer Portal	Quotations for Contracts, Notifications, CRM suggestions
Used equipment sales, balance inventory to demands	Ad-hoc as requested by buyers agents	Business intelligence

After Sumter's management team completes a simple gap analysis, they define a simple model of the business process that a particular project should provide. In the BPM/BR approach, business processes are independent of the systems and individual organizations that execute them, so the team builds a transition to the best solution even if the current systems cannot support the ideal business objective. The kinds of elements the team should explore in the ideal model should include the following:

- Identification of opportunities of process realignment
- Outsourcing
- Modernizations of activities
- Fine-tuning the results of mergers and reorganizations

The management team realized that the initial purchase of construction equipment is connected to the sale of aged equipment. Orders of new equipment should be matched with projected orders for leases for the time that Sumter Rents owns the equipment. The technical team realized that they should consolidate the entire process into a BI capability.

If your enterprise wants to initiate a BPM/BR, you will need to follow a clear and strategic method. Developing and completing a small pilot project with simple, achievable goals, and one or two limited services, is often a good way to get started. For instance, you might publish some important data for your clients to use. You might automate some legacy data processing functions with BPM (see Chapter 7). If you build some high-level business process diagrams, as I will do next, you might identify a possible pilot project. A pilot would allow you to test out the BPM/BR and see the results it provides before you fully commit to it. The business process diagrams should describe an area that has been targeted for improvement, upgrade, or alignment with goals. The pilot program may involve integrating one new software application, building a user application, or improving process management. One very important aspect of the pilot program is that it involves business and technical personnel.

Building   Top-level   Business   Process   Diagrams

Sumter Rents' managers have met, and they have developed a high-level business process for the customer and equipment parts of their business. As I mentioned earlier, developing a draft business process diagram (BPD) is a bit like whiteboard brainstorming. A BPD is not a *process flow* diagram. It is a representation of a long-running transaction (LRT). The shift from process flow to LRT is a critical idea in composite applications. Your programs provide the services that activities need to run. BPM design software manages the details and activity. The runtime calls them at the right moment. Think of each piece of rental equipment as a transaction that starts when the equipment enters their store inventory and is finished when it is sold, salvaged, or destroyed. Because it could be years before it is finished, this is a long-running transaction.

Figure 2.4 presents the central process for Sumter Rents—the equipment process. This process depicts equipment in the system as a LRT. It starts when equipment enters the inventory and ends when the equipment is either sold or destroyed. After equipment is entered into the inventory, it is entered in SAP PM if it has a maintenance schedule (SAP PM does not manage some items, such as hand tools and road barriers). After the staff checks in the equipment, they assign the equipment to a retail store. Now it is available for lease. At Sumter Rents' retail locations, the equipment cycles through customer leasing, and maintenance. It leaves the loop when the equipment either reaches its salvage age or Sumter Rents decides to sell it.

Let me explain the diagram a bit. Each business process diagram has a start (◌) and an end (◯). Activities are shown as boxes. Activities can be programs, Web services, or subprocesses. The lines denote the flow of information between the activities. Decisions are denoted with pointy boxes(⬦), while loops are shown as boxes and have a ? symbol on the left-hand side. There are more notations to be covered in the chapter on Business Process Management. These notations are similar to other business process modeling standards that have been developed.

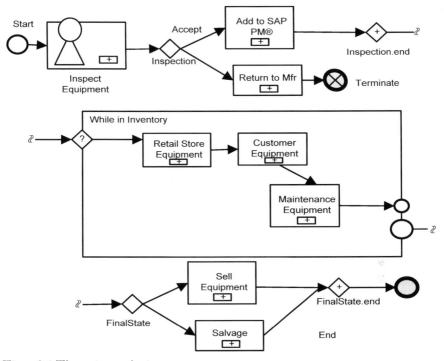

Figure 2.4 The equipment business process.

Because BPM software coordinates the activities, the business process approach simplifies the creation of applications. The programming team works with the code that performs the activities, and coordination is managed by the BPM software.

When I develop management-level abstract diagrams, I assume that every major activity is a subprocess. These are denoted with the + boxes in the lower half of the diagram. This way, I develop a list of business processes that must be completed in the business process modeling phase of the task.

The BPD shown in Figure 2.4 has sufficient detail for project planning. There are three important subprocesses that will need to be completed to meet our goals:

- Check equipment into store inventory
- Check the maintenance status of the equipment in SAP PM
- Lease the equipment to customers

Traditionally, most IT groups build separate customer applications and equipment applications. Even if they use a unified data model, the IT group writes code that orchestrates the two applications. With BPM, we discover the long-term business processes and build a business process diagram that runs. This is a better model of our business because it reduces the need to coordinate separate applications.

A PROJECT MANAGEMENT APPROACH IN A SIX SIGMA ORGANIZATION

Sumter's business management team defines its priorities by utilizing the Six Sigma method such as the one shown in Figure 2.5. This method identifies and prioritizes the short-term business problems that have clear benefits. These benefits might improve the productivity of organizations, such as transportation logistics or relationships with customers.

Project Definition for the Portfolio

In project definition, our management team selects projects that align business strategy with the present or future IT environment. During this step, they build a case for why a particular project should be done. To select a project, they define the problems and issues that they want to solve in the BPM/BR project portfolio. It might take many projects to modernize the entire architecture, yet each project should benefit the business. Earlier, we discussed the business architecture and decided the areas that needed alignment. This identified where to start. Now, we want to be more specific in defining the project.

Our team details the areas of business that need to be improved, as well as the areas that are helped with a better IT system. The questions they ask include: What are the business issues? What are the issues that remain from the current architecture? How can they be improved and made more efficient? Should a system be cut out?

:

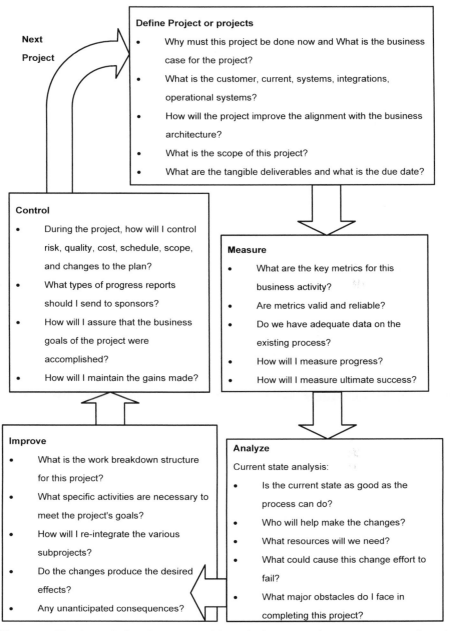

Figure 2.5 For Sumter's Six Sigma methodology, the business architecture activity is where the scope of the project is determined (Copyright © 2003 by Thomas Pyzdek).

For Sumter Rents, I will state the three project definitions and tasks as follows

Customer Lease Selection Improvements: The Six Sigma process definition bullets include:

- Why is the project needed now? To provide competitive levels of service to the largest customers, Sumter Rents needs to improve its Web-based customer service. Anecdotal evidence suggests that the company is losing income when customers have to wait for equipment from Sumter
- What are the highlights of the business case? We covered the key parts of the business case for the lease improvements earlier. Key economic drivers include an increasing use of heavy equipment leases by construction companies. The risk to the company is that they will lose sales volume to the competition with better customer support models
- The target customer is the construction contractor. Any group needing short- to medium-term leases, however, will benefit from these improvements
- The current Web system will need to be adjusted. The IT team will need to use the BPM software to connect the customer orders to SAP order entry. Several .NET parts will be needed
- The proposed project combines an improved customer support model and a .NET process spreadsheet. By creating a composite application that combines customer orders and project planning, the project will align with the business architecture
- The scope of the project is as follows: Sumter will develop a process for enrolling customers into a preferred group. The preferred group will be given access to special corporate discounts. They will receive a .NET spreadsheet that enables them to calculate the cost of the equipment leases in their project costs. The special Web services will also allow them to secure quotations for equipment operators. In addition, if the equipment they want is unavailable, the application will notify them when it is in a store near them
- The tangible deliverables for customer service improvements are: a new Web storefront, a Web-based process for customers to apply for preferred partner status, and .NET services to publish pricing and availability
- Sumter Management expects the project team to complete the project in three quarters

Internal Maintenance Management Process: Users access the SAP PM module through the thick client. SAP offers an iDOC to allow the state of the equipment to be posted as a Web service. When equipment is either checked in or at a predefined time interval, the software automatically reviews the maintenance status of the equipment. The Six Sigma process definition includes the following:

- There are two drivers for the immediacy of the maintenance management process improvement. First, not every organization uses SAP PM. This is especially true of the recently acquired stores. The result is that equipment is not always maintained according to the manufacturer's recommendations. Second, the manual process of entering data that triggers maintenance is prone to errors. The SAP PM system produces a few incorrect maintenance orders. The result of the mistaken orders is wasted clerical labor

- Highlights of business case: Equipment rental is the primary revenue generator for Sumter Rents. Because equipment is the largest capital expense, efficient and effective maintenance is one of the critical roles of Sumter Rents. Furthermore, the value of the aftermarket sales of equipment is strengthened by an aggressive maintenance regime. The purpose of this process is to improve and simplify this critical role. Currently, Sumter Rents is achieving a 93 percent compliance with the manufacturers' recommended maintenance schedule. The aim of the process improvement is to raise this to better than 99 percent. The long-term benefit to this project is an improved process that can be simultaneously published to all of Sumter's customers. It is hoped that the Web-based service will be a discriminator for customers. The benefit of the equipment maintenance contract is that the project will create revenue

- The customer of the maintenance process improvement is Sumter Rents' equipment managers. After the process has been proven, it will be part of the maintenance service contracts

- The current systems are the SAP PM and the Sumter Rents portal

- Equipment is the centerpiece of Sumter Rents' business. Sumter Rents is skilled in equipment maintenance. The project improves the alignment with the business architecture by improving the maintenance service of equipment

- The scope of this project is limited to automated maintenance scheduling in SAP PM.

- There are two deliverables in the scope of this project. The first is an Internet form to post equipment odometer readings to SAP PM. The second is a program that automatically pushes orders for maintenance to equipment managers

- The management expects the team to complete this project in six months

Balance Inventory and Used Equipment Sales: The sale of used equipment is a haphazard and inconsistent process. There are few standard policies for this practice and there are no automated reports or tools to aid stakeholders.

- Executive management aims to sell the optimum amount of used equipment while keeping a profitable inventory of new equipment. The current system is not as disciplined as it should be
- Highlights of the business case: Sales of used equipment is an important source of income and a mechanism for financing the modernization of Sumter Rents' fleet. Because determining the quantities of equipment to sell is complex, Sumter Rents is risking poor decisions in the used sales volumes and a less than optimal turnover in the inventory. The risk in the current process is unknown—the sales of used construction equipment might be better managed for more capital
- The customer of this project is the chief financial officer of Sumter Rents
- The system will need to need to build sales projections for the year. The system will need to gather data from some external sources. The project team will need to build interfaces with new equipment costs from manufacturers
- There are no commercially available solutions for this problem. The native capabilities of BI tools, however—including *dash boards* and business activity monitoring—play a role in this application
- This project aims to increase the quality of the inventory. It does so by balancing the used equipment sales with projected business revenue. The project improves the alignment with the business architecture
- The scope of this project is limited to decision support for the equipment sales problem
- The tangible deliverable is a construction of a BI solution
- The management expects the team to complete this project in six months

As a project is started, the management team performs project management. A selected project becomes part of a project portfolio that is monitored and fine-tuned.

Measure. As a BPM/BR project progresses, the management team monitors the progress. Software projects are often measured in terms of function points, and these are usually very technical. The ultimate success of the BPM/BR project happens after the technical work is completed, and the metrics that drive the business change.

The benefits of these three projects should yield tangible increases in business performance metrics. The customer process improvement should increase rental sales to construction customers. The customer process will be built with measurements of the number of follow-on sales that occur after a customer is notified that the equipment he needed is available. SAP PM monitors the compliance with manufacturers' maintenance regimens. An improvement in the maintenance function should improve this metric. Lastly, BI in the equipment sales areas should improve the revenue of the operation.

Analyze. As the project proceeds, its status should be analyzed for the quality of its progress. When management closely monitors the quality of the project, they avoid potential failures and obstacles to success.

Improve Over time. The managers view the projects in aggregate and may merge portions of the projects.

Control. The project sponsor controls the risks, quality, cost schedule, and changes to the program. These activities are the chief business architecture tools that move the enterprise into alignment with its goals.

Finally, security is an increasingly key consideration in the business architecture of the enterprise. Business security should consider the sensitivity of operations and data. The enterprise must protect its data assets and intellectual property. Increasingly, government and customer relationships mandate a model for protecting data privacy.

The output of the business architecture includes the structure of the business processes that the organization is working toward, independent of the existing systems and practices. This architecture is an ideal that the organization is striving for. The BPM/BR creates systems that are characterized by a loose coupling of the business process and the systems that support it. From this ideal, projects are selected that implement the corporate vision. Other outputs of this activity are the selected projects, business use cases for the projects, and a set of tasks and deliverables. During this activity, each of the projects is monitored as a portfolio.

BUSINESS ARCHITECTURE DISCUSSION

The first activity of the BPM/BR is analyzing the business architecture. Here is where we explore and discover new initiatives for services to be published and used. Where is the business in the information chain? What areas of the business should be outsourced to more efficient areas? In this activity, the BPM/BR addresses the strategic and tactical goals of the business. This should be old hat for business executives, but what is new is the application of BPM in reengineering their processes for competitive reasons. Business architecture in the BPM/BR provides a new type of systems integration for the strategies and objectives of management. The outcome of the business architecture analysis is a portfolio of projects that should obliterate the IT-Business divide.

Executive managers understand that information systems are a critical supporting part of every modern business strategy. They direct and support these systems with an eye on the value of corporate investment in technology. The BPM/BR process provides this value these ways:

- Raising the complexity and scope of the problems that are tackled by the merging of business processes and business rules
- Publishing the native capabilities in an innovative way will raise an organization's agility
- Easily tuning and configuring processes, cutting the time needed to change a business rule or process

Many types of changes that formerly needed programming are cut. Because of BPM/BR's focus on BI, managers have ready access to the critical information they need.

A strategic goal of most corporate management models is to align the best, or most profitable, business practices with the process model. Some of these new practices need complex, atomic decisions about data. For instance, customers essentially create their own rules and processes in CRM. Highly sophisticated international transactions need sophisticated models for developing currency factors. Predicting the failure of systems pits the wholesale application of data mining techniques against large volumes of data. These complexities often need tuning.

More often your organization solves problems by fine-tuning metrics and key performance indicators. These are tactical things. At this level, you are measuring what is looming, what we are doing well, what we are, how we can get more out of the business, and what type of cross-selling we can do? How can we improve the percentage of our target customers?

Either strategically or tactically, management leadership sets goals and objectives that should be measured over time or in terms of milestones.

Executive-level planning like this often leads to changes in the supporting business systems: a business activity is outsourced, a new offering is made to customers, or trading partners are added. This is where BPM/BR fits in. It will develop projects that support these goals and objectives.

The BPM/BR supports many of these new integration needs. Some business architecture initiatives that might affect business systems at the process level include:

- Improving understanding of customer behavior
- Providing managers with better support systems
- Cutting the cost of purchasing; bundling purchase agreements
- Outsourcing operations such as human resources, customer finance, shipping, or manufacturing
- Changing financial practices such as payment on receipt of materials
- Putting into effect government-mandated regulations, including mandated disclosures, and environmental, health, and safety regulations
- Gaining better intelligence on real-time data, predictive failures, data mining, and occult patterns that change yet yield informed decisions

BPM/BR projects are an outgrowth of the basic planning of the initiatives that it takes to meet these goals.

I look at business architecture as the building blocks that create and support the success of the organization. Components might range from the abstract (such as the capability to foresee business opportunities), to the concrete (such as manufacturing capability). The composite of these form a business' most detailed strategy. These building blocks are linked and supported by streams of information. Adding a new block to the stack always influences communications and often needs the type of enterprise application integration (EAI) that is supported by the BPM/BR.

In the BPM/BR, the first part of the business architecture activity is for the BPM/BR management team to inventory the building blocks of the organization's activities and then contrast the activities with the current IT environment. This is limited to the building blocks that surround an initiative. Parts of the resources of the business are the large-scale systems such as ERP, human resources, logistics, and others.

From this first sketch of the problem and the areas that it touches, the BPM/BR team should define an abstract or a virtual model of the business process that a project or groups of projects should provide. As with the BPM concept, the BPM/BR business architecture strives for an ideal model of business processes—one that is independent of the systems that are operating the business.

The aim of the analysis part of the business architecture is to define a project that aligns business strategy with the present, or future, IT environment.

CEO-level initiatives often create portfolios of projects needed to create the result. Portfolios might be managed vertically—assigned to areas of finance, engineering, or IT—or horizontally, by objectives. In summary, it is important in your project definition for you to write a business case for the project. In finalizing the project plans, the team should outline the current systems involved—the integration elements, operational systems, and analytical or data warehouses. If the project requires the upgrade or substantial retrofit of a legacy system, the BPM/BR team should determine whether a COTS solution is available. When COTS is available, then an independent return-on-investment (ROI) analysis should be developed.

Armed with a business case and ROI, the team will have an objective case for how the project improves alignment with the business architecture. After they select a project, they develop the scope, tangible deliverables, and due date for the project. A project sponsor is a team member or members that are responsible for the completion of the project. This is not, however, the end of their involvement in the subsequent activities.

The SOA strives for an ideal model of business processes—one that is independent of the systems that are currently operating the business. The SOA evolves over time. With an SOA approach, organizations expose small portions of the current system architecture as a service and move towards the target business architecture.

SUMMARY

* Business architecture describes the basic building blocks of an enterprise, including strategies, tactics, and the infrastructure to be built.

* You use business processes to align tactics and strategies with the organization and technical infrastructure. The high-level business processes become candidates for project definition.

* In project definition, you clarify the need and set up the scope, deliverables, and time frames for the project.

* We defined three projects in our case study. These are:

    * Create an improved equipment maintenance process. The purpose of this project is to simplify maintenance of equipment with SAP PM. The improved process will be offered to customers as a service.

- Create a closer relationship with commercial customers by improving their rental experience and simplifying the chore of estimating construction project details.

- Create a more precise method for deciding what quantity of equipment to sell on the open market. This method will use BI technology.

REFERENCES

Karmarkar, Uday, 2004. "Will You Survive the Services Revolution? " Boston, MA, Harvard Business Review.

CHAPTER THREE: BUSINESS PROCESS MANAGEMENT

When a customer fills out an order for something on a Website, he has completed only one process step from the perspective of the business. The enterprise has not done its work with the order until the business rules approve the customer, the order entry system supplies the order, the ERP's accounts payable module is called, and perhaps a work flow system sends an email. In BPM jargon, this is known as a long-running transaction (LRT). In a BPM approach, these steps are activities. Different organizations and different systems complete the LRT. For instance, the company with the Web site may have outsourced some steps. Someone has to ship the box, so some steps are manual. Each system that performs the computer work of the process is one activity or unit of work.

You and your team should start to develop a project's business processes by setting up its objectives. Building this is a progression from the objectives to the sequence of activity steps. This will build what I call the core business process (CBP). The CBP is independent of the COTS applications that perform accounting and other roles.

The questions the team should ask itself are: What is the scope of the process? What are the steps that the process must finish in order for the business to reach its goal? Next, the analysts define what data the LRT should gather and how it will provide this data to the specific systems that need it. You develop this by cataloging the data and services needed by the systems and mapping this to the core process activities and data.

The BR becomes important where the processes start to enforce policies. Business rules need to convert, manipulate, or corroborate the data. The most common examples are decisions about the validity of the data that is entering an activity in the process. If a user has not correctly entered a form or transaction, the process must return an error to the requester. If the business process branches to manage subprocesses, then the rules might decide this. I am going to describe where you place the business rules into an activity on the diagram. The activity will then be linked to a Web service for the business rules portion of the activity. The benefit of the composite process occurs when these business rules change. For instance, if you change a decision that accepts or rejects data, then the process itself will not need to change.

Our project portfolio aligns Sumter Rents' business systems with strategies for customers and equipment. We aim to build business processes for Sumter Rents that will carry out needed business tactics as long-running transactions (LRTs). They touch many systems, yet, for Sumter Rents, they are the basic transactions of the business.

A business process diagram (BPD) depicts an iteration of an LRT. BPM software allows you to oversee the progress of the transaction as it moves through the process. For instance, the equipment process for a bulldozer may endure for years. Earlier, I made the analogy that a business process diagram is similar to a process flow diagram. What is different is the information within the lines between the activities. Each activity has the ability to calculate, assign, or delete downstream data with upstream values. A transaction in a business process is like one sheet from a clipboard of business forms. The process manipulates and stores all the information. The BPD design tools define what actions take place on the data sets. Business model symbols include ingenuous activity types, schedulers, and flow control. Flow control includes switches (if ... then ... else) and others that simplify the control of the data in the business process. Think of the business process diagram as a factory that acts on the business forms in an assembly line process.

I mentioned that business processes are like process flow diagrams. They are also atomic, however, like a single set of related business records. They represent an instance of the business process. Think of my example of the equipment process. The diagram itself applies to the single unit. For each of the equipment units that Sumter Rents owns—a bulldozer, a motorized lift—there is an instance of the equipment process. This is the power of the BPEL engine. Obviously, if every piece of equipment has an instance of a business process then you could build queries of the BPEL engine. You could discover how many units need maintenance today? How many customers have rented bulldozers of type x today?

As your team develops the business process, it should look for areas where policies and data support important decisions. This is where the business rules connect to the process as a service. I suggest that you perform your evaluations with business rules if the process that you are modeling is raising an event or selecting a path in the process flow by:

- Computing conditions across historical data
- Sorting and classifying a process based on numeric causes
- Querying an operational data store for historical events

If you have connected your business process with a service that invokes the rule, then you can easily change the basis for the decision or event.

BUSINESS RULES WORK WITHIN BUSINESS PROCESSES

The choice of what should become a business rule, and what should become a part of the process, is not difficult. Consider my earlier statement that business rules mediate the data's content. Business rules should use data to support decisions, and the process should direct that data to the services that consume it or provide other data. Table 3.1 presents some general guidelines for what to carry out as business rules and what to include in the process.

Table 3.1 This table lists some guidelines for what should be a part of the business process and what should be a part of the business rules repository.

Design Item	Example	Process or Rule
Decision	If customer is preferred then develop greatest discount	Business Rule
Policy	Equipment is sent to retail store under certain conditions	Business Rule
Post to application service	SAP PM®	Business Process
State, duration, or location of entity	Equipment in maintenance, assigned to customer or at retail store	Business Process
Direct data to branch of process	Decisions, while loop, subprocess	Business Process
Read external transaction	Customer equipment on maintenance contract	Business Process
Certify external transaction	Confirm attributes of a transaction	Business Rule
Report data errors to external system	Errors in business rule approval	Business Process
Reference data	Customer's credit limit	Business Rule or Business Process
Convert process data to interface	Mapping accounting transactions for ERP	Business Rule or Business Process
Store data in operational data store	Record the clerical details of an order	Business Rule or Business Process

The business process diagram is often a complex map of flow control. It will have many subprocesses, decisions, and *while loops*. Wherever a decision or while loop appears, you should consider the basis for the change in flow. The business rules should evaluate the data provided by the process. Next, the business rule should provide control to the process so it can make a decision. This is the best use of business rules in the business process.

The last three examples are *gray areas*. If there are changing means of gaining reference data for a process, and it provides important process parameters for decisions, then you should consider this a business rule. If the reference data are information that the process needs for sequencing or scheduling data, then you might not need the business rules approach. Mapping process parameters into the data needed by an interface is another requirement you might design as a business rule. Business rules are an effective way of managing data when there are a lot of changes in the database.

Finally, if systems outside the business process environment need data, then either business rules or process engines store operational data. BPMN engines might populate operational data during an instance of a process.

SUMTER'S NEW PROCESSES

During business process modeling, a BPM/BR technical/management team creates or tunes a business process model that supports the project's objectives. What are the mental processes of the team members developing business processes and connecting business rules? They use workshops and communication. They interview the best-performing and the worst-performing actors in the processes. They review documentation and the notes of the managers of the current process. They identify business rules and the process needs for policies or chose proper flow control.

There are institutional or traditional ways of gathering information. Sumter Rents has reams of paper, cabinets full of files, and databases overflowing with useful information—from management directives to marketing papers to MIS memorandums. Much important information exists here. Yet, business process modeling is different from data modeling. The purpose of data modeling is to develop a model of *what is*. The purpose of business process modeling is to develop a model of *what should be*.

A PROCESS FOR BUSINESS PROCESS MODELING

Figure 3.1 presents a process for modeling business processes. Core process areas are those areas that are essential to a business process, yet independent of the systems that service their needs. If the team needs to design or adjust a core business process, they will do that first. If the only change is to an interface, then they create and adjust the interface processes.

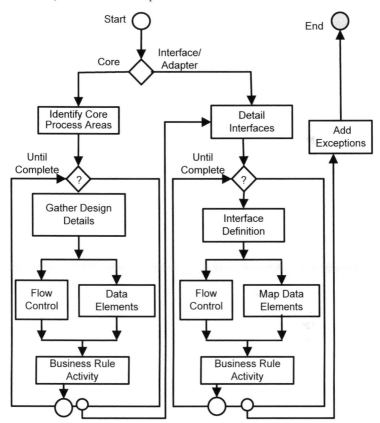

Figure 3.1 The design team creates the business process; an iterative process of developing activities, connecting them with flow control and mediating the flow with business rules.

I have used a *while loop* to show the development of a business process. The next activity is to the gather design details that create a business process design. Design details include use cases for user interfaces or system interfaces. As the team gathers details, they may need to design Web screens to collect data. They develop file formats or XML transactions that the business process will read.

Flow controls connect the design details, which become process activities. When the activity needs some external services, it calls a partner application.

After flow controls, the team develops the data—or business entities for the business process. Most business processes route an entire business form.

For core business processes and interfaces, the design team will add business rules to the diagram. They evaluate important flow controls to identify subject areas for business rules. Within the process, at the suitable location, the rules carry out policy, constraints, or competitive business practices.

In the BPM activity, teams document the workflow of the process steps with BPM software. The process workflow describes the critical path. This includes activities and subprocesses that are run in parallel, or those that are sequential. If the team is working on several business processes, they may need to develop interprocess orchestrations. Afterwards, they might discover opportunities to design a more efficient process.

The final step of the business process is for the project team to define likely exceptions and points of failure. Business processes should be able to recover from reasonable system failures. The project team may need to define compensations, or what to do if the business process must remove a transaction.

The outcome of business process design should be a working process prototype. The prototype corroborates working interfaces and confirms business entities.

A Concept Diagram for the Business Process

Figure 3.2 depicts the concepts of the process shown in Figure 3.1 by connecting the business process and the business rules ideas beneath and within the process definition.

An organization's processes can be classified into material processes, information processes, and business processes. A material process is the assembly or delivery of physical products. Information processes outline the automated, and partly automated, tasks that create, manage, and provide information. A business processes is a market-centered description of an organization's activities. A business uses business rules to create policies, guidelines, negotiations, and offerings. This is how the business process is controlled and provided with critical information. The figure below merges these two methods:

The process definition is the *centroid* of the diagram. The activities in the process description may be fully automated, or may involve humans interacting with computers. BPMN models automated processes. BPEL directs the detail of the processes, and is arguably the most prevalent way to describe automated business processes. It describes—in a XML specification language—the activities that need to be performed, the participants (partners) who could or should perform them, and the interdependencies that exist among them (flow control). BPEL simplifies describing processes, their tasks, and the dependencies among the tasks. One of these services may be a rules service, which is a Web service that invokes a call to a business rule.

Prominent BPM software, such as Intalio, and Tibco, provide libraries of services. These services are partners, and they are added to your BPEL when you add them to the diagram. Examples of these services are messaging services, file utilities, and Web user interfaces. BPM software also provides prepackaged services for ERPs. These are known as *adapters*.

On the right branch of the diagram in Figure 3.2, business processes are managed to completion. BPM software should carry out the BPEL process description—assigning the proper activity to the responsible system or person. For example, the software may assign manual activities and access to the software tools needed to finish the task. These tools might include databases, spreadsheets, and design software. Another role of BPM software is to issue dependencies among the tasks. Finally, the BPM software should support multiple invocations (instances) of a given process and a given task.

Examine the left side of the concept diagram. The business rules engine controls the instances of business rules. By manipulating the rules schema, you control the flow of activities in a business process. A service invoked by the business process carries out the business rules. The concept diagram shows this as a *rules service*, which is an internal system. In Chapter 4, I will describe the rules schema, which is a part of the business rules repository. The rules schema defines the WSDL that specifies the binding for the business process.

Business processes work with flows of data. You might think of these flows as (paper) business forms that move from place to place, person to person. Customer orders or equipment repair tickets are examples. The process is a conduit for one or more of these forms to flow in its designated path. The data comes from outside the business process—either from another system or from a message sent by another business process. The business rule uses the data in the business form to direct the business process. Business rules should correct, certify, and mediate every data item the business uses. Business rules create or encourage special behavior. Separating these two ideas allows an organization to change the decisions without complex changes in computer code.

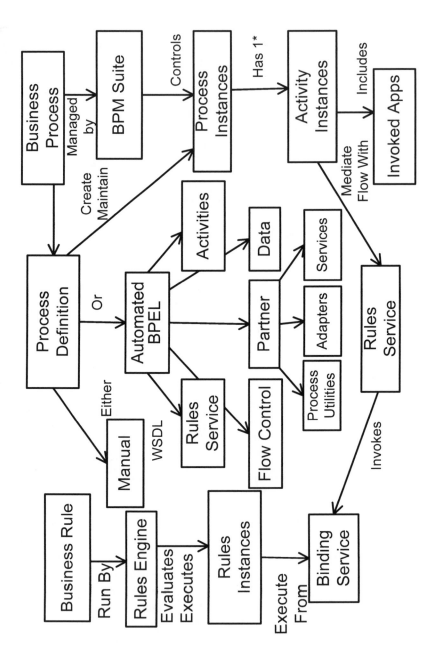

Figure 3.2 A concept decomposition of business rules and business processes with interacting ideas and subject areas. I will describe the specification for the rules service in the next chapter.

Scheduling is a critical part of BPM. However, processes drive the business rules that trigger events. For instance, imagine the process that a business needs to *dun* a customer. The business rules should define intensifying processes for contacting a customer about a tardy payment. We are going to describe a similar requirement for equipment processes. A process must often check the maintenance schedule to determine when the equipment must be serviced. Business rules will decide how critical the maintenance is when a customer schedules it.

Lying between the users and operational systems should be the business rules that the enterprise controls—including the stovepipes and the ERP. Special offerings and fine-tuning of the business transactions to increase the yields and offer better customer service is the domain of the business rule. You might even call a CRM system a set of business rules for the individual customer to use. For instance, a rule might set up communications with a customer that would like to rent a particular product. For Sumter Rents, the customer would want to know when equipment is available at a variety of locations.

EQUIPMENT MAINTENANCE PROCESS IMPROVEMENTS

The equipment process is the most important part of Sumter Rents' business. The process starts with the purchase of equipment, and ends with its sale or disposal. Along the way, customers lease it, and the company maintains it with a schedule controlled by SAP PM. We are going to create these processes, and show how BPM software simplifies the steps of gathering the needed data and controls.

Sumter Rent's management has appointed a small team to develop these processes. They gather information from reading standard procedures and visiting equipment managers at stores.

Because personnel suggest that the maintenance management is complicated, the team wants to discover the complexity of it all. They hope to find the underlying issues in interviews with the staff. The design team orally describes the process. In one discussion about the current equipment process, an equipment manager described his view by stating that managers are responsible for four activities:

- Receiving and inspecting new equipment. If there are inspection issues, he is responsible for resolving the issues
- Preparing the equipment for issue to rental customers
- Getting the equipment from the customer after use. He inspects the equipment for damage. He checks the equipment back into rental inventory
- Carrying out scheduled maintenance for the equipment

The evidence of a broken process was everywhere.

This list suggests some starting points for the activities and some decision points and business rules in the business process.

During the interview, the process team notes that the manager keeps much of his information on clipboards and in notes. In more detailed interviews, they discover that the equipment manager has been running maintenance reports on the store's inventory. The team asks why the manager needs so much data. The managers respond that most equipment maintenance occurs because the hours on the odometer have exceeded a threshold value. There are other conditions that call for maintenance, and the current SAP PM process is only designed for equipment that is on the lot of the retail store, not assigned to a customer.

The questions about the clipboard's data identify several important process issues. With large store inventories, the conditions that cause or trigger preventive maintenance might be unwieldy. Occasionally, the store issues equipment to customers just before the scheduled inventory or a manufacturer recall. For instance, imagine that a dangerous defect is discovered in a piece of heavy equipment. Sumter would want to collect this equipment from the customer immediately. When the equipment is off site for an extended time, the maintenance schedule might lapse. Sometimes Sumter leases equipment to customers without going through the check-in process. So, to avoid losing maintenance cycles, the managers keep long printouts of the maintenance schedules of the equipment. An aim of the business process team is to reduce these difficulties with a more accurate process.

At this early phase of business process modeling, the team collects basic process and data features from the activities around the project. Important data for the equipment manager includes the equipment identifiers and the acceptance dates. Manufacturers provide the maintenance regimes—including start-up procedures—through SAP PM. The philosophy is a bit different than traditional use case analysis. The purpose of BPM is to discover what *should* be done, not what *is* done.

The process team is now able to add more detail to the high-level diagrams that were created in the business architecture phase of the project.

As shown in the business process in Figure 3.3, our teams add process activities and decisions after interviewing the equipment manager. I have split the diagram out from top to bottom. The symbol (?) marks a continuity with the process flow from the upper right-hand side. You should examine these diagrams and connect the notation on them to the interview discoveries. The equipment inspection might result in a return to the manufacturer for correction or replacement, and the team has added a decision to support this. If the local manager accepts the equipment, then SAP PM assigns an equipment identifier to the unit. After the equipment manager has accepted the unit, he might need to perform start-up procedures. The business process should immediately call these out.

The process assigns the equipment to store inventory, and the while loop starts. Figure 3.3 shows the use of a message queue within the while loop. The equipment state message activity includes:

- Sending the process to the customer subprocess. The customer application has assigned it to a customer
- Sending the process to a retail store. By default, Sumter Rents may move the equipment from store to store
- Sending the process to maintenance if maintenance is warranted
- Exiting the loop, if Sumter decides to remove the equipment from inventory

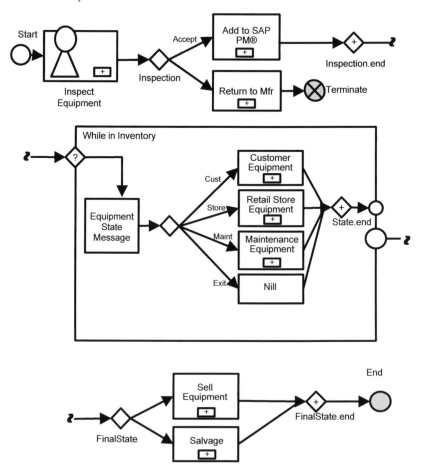

Figure 3.3 This business process diagram depicts a more detailed equipment process. A message queue controls the flow.

On this and future business process diagrams, my goal is to show a portion of what a BPM solution looks like. I have condensed some activities, such as the user activity on the left side of Figure 3.3. In practice, the Inspect Equipment workflow activity would entail more steps than merely hanging a Web screen from a business process diagram. A user interface would need some process coordination. The process shown in Figure 3.3 is missing activities that assign values to the data in the process flows.

Conditions continually check for maintenance in the equipment process. This is why we have chosen a message-driven solution for managing the state of the equipment. Messages communicate with all the processes. Four different factors drive the SAP maintenance schedule: age of ownership, equipment hours, manufacturers' recall, and changing seasons. These causes are independent of where the equipment is in the process—equipment managers cannot depend on the equipment being in the yard to perform maintenance. The process needs to respond to these events asynchronously. In any high-level activity, the process should check for a maintenance event. This means that there are different events that call for equipment maintenance: the odometer reading on the unit has reached a certain value, a particular period of time has passed, or a change in the seasons or a manufacturer's recall has occurred. Because time-based changes occur intermittently, we will need the system to be looking for these events in the background.

The *customer equipment* subprocess is presented in Figure 3.4. The process continues in a loop until it receives a message that the customer has returned the equipment to a retail store.

In the assigned equipment process, the first activity looks at the message queue for equipment returned by the customer. An application sends the message when the equipment arrives at the retail store. Perhaps a PDA reads a bar code on the equipment. When the equipment has been returned, the process next calls the equipment check-in subprocess, which checks for the presence of a maintenance message. If one exists, the process will flag the equipment's status as *needing maintenance* and call the business rule to decide if personnel must bring the equipment into the shop.

Finally, the process returns to the main equipment process. The process will direct the equipment to either the retail store process or the maintenance process.

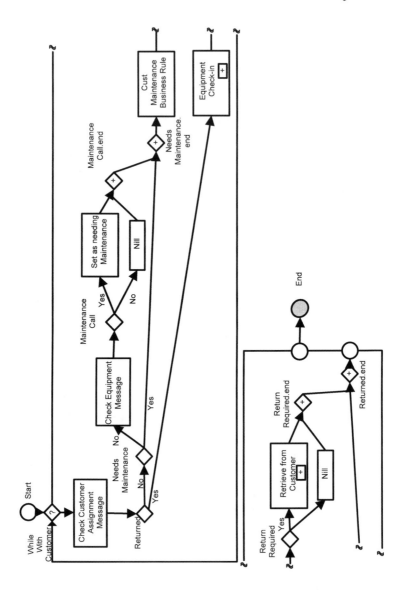

Figure 3.4 This business process diagram depicts the customer assignment subprocess from Figure 3.3. It shows how the maintenance events affect the customer assigned equipment.

These processes should be as independent from the means of data entry as possible. This will allow Sumter Rents to develop new ways of entering the data. For instance, at a future date, radio frequency identification (RFID) may perform equipment return. You achieve independence from the method of data collection by using messaging tactics.

Equipment Entities

The purpose of the equipment process is to oversee and control the location of the equipment and to hold the data that SAP PM will need to decide when maintenance is due. Equipment is either at a retail location, assigned to a customer, or is in maintenance. The service history is a list of the odometer readings and date values for the equipment. Retail stores inspect the equipment when it is received from the customers or when it is sent from another retail location. The equipment process works with a simple entity—the equipment business entity object. The logical information diagram for this is shown in Figure 3.5.

Figure 3.5 The equipment process uses the equipment entity to manage the state and location of a piece of equipment.

In an effort to be concise, I have not shown the attributes of the equipment information. The equipment process creates an instance of the equipment form and its fields in the first activity in Figure 3.3.

Even though Sumter Rents is using SAP PM, they maintain a separate catalog of equipment in an *operational datastore* for use across the enterprise. The operational datastore is a database of information that is independent of the commercial applications. The equipment catalog will be useful in other processes and applications, particularly the data warehouse.

Offering Equipment Maintenance Services

The BPM suite enables Sumter Rents to offer the equipment maintenance process to their customers as a product. The process design team has designed an equipment maintenance process that is independent of the larger Sumter Rents equipment process. By exposing the equipment maintenance service as an external process, Sumter Rents can offer this to their customers.

The process team designs the customer's contract service to use SAP PM through the existing maintenance process. It accepts the same data—mileage or hours on the equipment. The top-level of the contract maintenance process is presented in Figure 3.3. The team has designed the different steps for the equipment for the entire life of the customer contract. In the first step, a separate application enters the customer's equipment into SAP PM. There is a customer contract and billing process and the equipment only exists for the life of the contract. The process may also renew a customer's contract.

After the process enters a customer's contracted equipment into the system, the service part of the process loop may begin. The process in Figure 3.6 depends on a message that it receives from a process that looks at equipment in SAP PM. For instance, if the maintenance department must lubricate the equipment every six months, this business process will notify the customer and the service manager of this need in a timely manner.

Figure 3.6 This business process diagram depicts how the Sumter Rents Maintenance Service uses the common equipment maintenance process that broadcasts a message to this process.

The business process also offers important services for the maintenance customers who want a history of work that has already been done on the equipment. This maintenance history increases the value of Sumter's capital investment because it increases the resale value of the equipment.

Sumter Rents' executives knew there was profit in offering equipment maintenance to their customers, and the efficiency of the SAP PM system impressed their customers. To do it efficiently, however, the new business process would need to give customers the same service as the retail outlets. By unifying business strategy with technology, the BPM in Figure 3.6 creates new product offerings and opportunities for outsourcing.

Business Rules Subject Areas in Equipment

Because SAP handles decisions about equipment areas, there are surprisingly few business rules in the equipment process. The business process for equipment needs to manage the following decisions:

- When the schedule calls for maintenance of equipment that is assigned to customers, Sumter needs to decide when the customer should return the equipment for service. This might apply to customers who have leased the equipment for long periods of time
- When the manufacturer recalls equipment for safety defects, the process must decide when the recall warrants retrieval from the customer

- When the customer returns equipment, the process should validate the data on the check-in form. Much of the maintenance is based on odometer hours. Because it is easy for the equipment technician to make an error in entering usage hours, business rules should routinely look at and verify this data
- The business process needs a business rule to map the equipment attributes to the SAP PM iDoc attributes

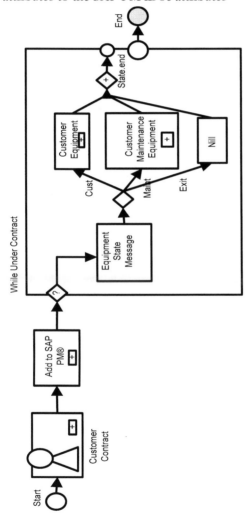

The process design team may begin the business rules approach for these topics, or detail them later. If there is a separate team developing the business rules, then they model the business rules with activity placeholders on the BPD

(Figure 3.4 shows one of these business rules). Their placement is consistent with my introductory remarks about the use of the rule to control flow in the business process.

To unit test the business process, the process designers put hard-coded, or dummy, business rules into the process flow.

CUSTOMER RELATIONSHIP PROCESS

Despite a solid ERP implementation, many of Sumter Rents' retail processes are manual. Store personnel assign equipment to walk-in customers using a paper form. Large commercial customers want a more modern process, so the business process team works with the marketing team to develop the customer ordering process.

The marketing team wants to use a combination of the Web model of the rental car industry, and the shopping cart of popular retail Web pages. These two popular features serve as a model for the new customer relationship process. Customers will be able to choose the equipment types that they wish to rent, and select the dates they wish to lease them. If the units are unavailable on the desired dates, the system will ask them if they wish to receive an email when the equipment is available. The customer may also choose to have Sumter Rents deliver the equipment to his location.

The customer business process is presented in Figure 3.7. The process reserves available equipment for the rental period and places the selected equipment in their shopping cart. The folio prices the equipment and mobilization charges, taking into account special discounts to preferred customers using the customer discount rule. When the customer has completed his folio, he reserves the folio. The reservation is secured with a credit card—or, if he is a preferred customer, he needs no further data.

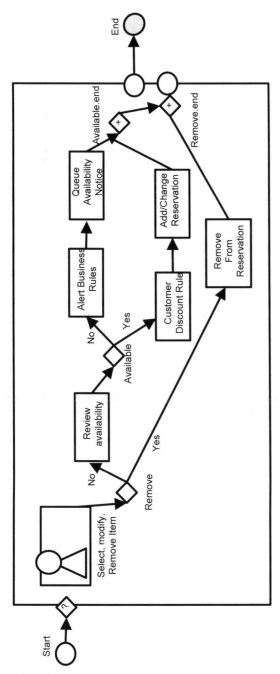

Figure 3.7 This business process diagram depicts the Sumter Rents customer folio system.

Figure 3.7 presents another example of an LRT. This diagram shows how the BPM method reduces programming. In a database-centric model, the state of the process would be stored in transactions. For instance, a developer might hold the details of a reservation in a table with status flags. Business process software keeps the list of equipment, thereby cutting the programming associated with user interfaces.

I have not presented all the processes needed for the customer service application. Sumter Rents hopes to develop a preferred customer program to build loyalty with its largest customers. Therefore, it will need a process for identifying such customers, and another for accepting applications. The BI chapter will describe the method for defining which customers are candidates for *preferred* status.

A better business process should improve customer loyalty. Construction firms prepare quotations for competitive bids and job estimates. A bid is won or lost on a small margin, so each bid needs to contain accurate costs. In the business architecture phase, the management team suggested publishing a spreadsheet with a .NET Web service component as a customer rental process. The spreadsheet allows the customer to link real-time rental costs to their bids when preparing budgets.

The customer process allows them to build a folio of requested equipment that remains open as long as the customer has equipment out on lease. This is another long-running transaction. The customer service process adds and removes equipment to the job folio so that costs are separated according to jobs. Sumter bills the customer monthly for the equipment, according to the charges within the folio.

Customer Entities

The data concept diagram for the customer process is shown in Figure 3.8. The concept depicts the data design that occurs during the BPM design process.

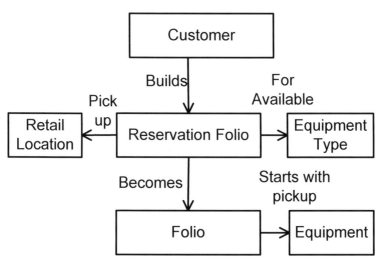

Figure 3.8 The customer process uses the customer folio entities to manage large commercial orders for the rental of equipment.

The customer form contains the data needed to build a reservation. Preferred customers have a negotiated discount that applies to the total value of the reservation. After a reservation is made, customers are assigned the equipment of the type specified in the reservations folio.

Relations with the Equipment Process

There is an important relationship between the customer process and the equipment process. Earlier, we described a subprocess that assigns equipment to customers. The customer process tells the equipment process what equipment the store has assigned to the customer. This message style of interface allows the two processes to exist independently. This independence allows the business to make changes to the process flow.

Customer service is a part of both the equipment process and the customer process. There are conditions that compel servicing of equipment while the customer has it. For instance, Sumter Rents would want to bring back equipment that is out on lease if it has been the subject of a safety recall. Sumter also needs to perform critical maintenance on equipment that is out on longer leases.

It is important for processes to be *loosely bound* and able to post events that communicate with other processes. Separating the processes positions them for change. A BPM suite should be able to change the processes while completing the ones that are in existence.

Business Rules Subject Areas in Customer Service

Sumter Rents aims to influence customer behavior by creating a responsive service process. These rules control the process:

- A business rule will get a customer's preferred status and apply the greatest appropriate discount to the reservation
- A business rule will decide if the customer has requested an email notice or a phone notice if the needed equipment is at a nearby retail location
- A business rule will map entries from the business process attribute into the SAP accounts payable iDOC
- A business rule will find out if auxiliary equipment is needed based on all the equipment in the folio. The process application will suggest that they order the equipment.

The activities for two of these rules are shown in the customer process as Alert Business Rule and Customer Discount Rule.

SUMMARY OF OUR BUSINESS PROCESS MODELING ACTIVITIES

During business process design, the earlier rapid markups we built (if any) in the architecture phase become more complex. As we develop more detail, we add more flow control symbols to the diagram. These symbols represent the flow, steps, and conditions of the business. For instance, we discovered in the interview that different schedules and events cause maintenance on the equipment. BPMN depicts a schedule as a small clock. The schedule looks in SAP PM to see if there is any maintenance needed and, if so, sends a message to the equipment process that treats the message as a multiple event queue. The message decides the suitable process path.

BPMN produces the BPEL that the engine uses to perform the process. BPMN/BPEL coordinates activities and events in a new and effective way. In the equipment example, we needed a message-driven event that wakes up every day, or hour, to look for scheduled equipment maintenance events. With each new equipment state, a subprocess queries SAP PM for the maintenance events. From that point forward, the event message communicates the maintenance schedule to the equipment process. This is all self-contained within the equipment LRT. With older programming methods, creating a message-event activity required advanced programming techniques. COTS products, such as SAP PM, manage equipment maintenance regimes well, but getting the information events to the field is complex without BPMN.

DEVELOPING THE CORE BUSINESS PROCESS (CBP)

Every enterprise runs its business models through a series of Core Business Processes. I have described how some of Sumter Rents business processes support the core business architecture. These include the equipment process and the customer process. Other obvious processes are in the areas of accounting and human resources. These are the core processes that define their business.

A core business process is different from a traditional data or system process. In the past, we would create a program to send a database transaction in a flat file to an ERP. Much of the development was about the mysterious needs of the target system, and the details of the process were buried in the details of the integration. The program code did the mappings of the source attributes. The core business process is all about what the business does, irrespective of these details.

Core processes are independent of the systems that fulfill them. A traditional system is built to process specific procedures within a system, and these procedures process data and create transactions and reports. A CBP performs a goal or an activity within the business architecture. The CBP uses the application as a service that moves transactions or queues a procedure within a system.

There is another important difference: the CBP does its work through process data. The benefit of this is that managers and process administrators work with the specific instances of a process—a customer's order or a specific contract order. In a traditional system, this may be a query or a report. It is not a native feature of the environment. BPM strengthens the traditional business data with descriptive process information, especially timing information for activities.

When we want them to be more efficient and controllable, core processes change internally. Enterprises use BPM to fine-tune the process and make them more efficient, so even the flow controls may change. There are long-term benefits for a business that uses a core process approach. By identifying core business processes, it is easier to position a service or product for outsourcing. Legacy systems often lock important processes in a milieu of databases and point-to-point integration. This is the problem of many legacy processes, especially in government. For instance, if transportation is not the work of a COBOL mainframe program, then you can outsource your transportation needs. A core process approach unlocks your processes and positions them for worthwhile change.

As information (think of business forms) flows through a business process, every activity, decision, scope, or loop may use any of the upstream process attributes (form fields). Activities have inputs and outputs. As the information flows along the process, an activity may use the inputs or the outputs to calculate, decide, or transform information. Diverting the data into a separate, late-binding business rules service creates more flexibility for improving business execution.

In the future, advanced organizations will view their core processes and business rules as some of their most important assets. These core processes will need stewardship. Advanced enterprises will carefully tune the basic business processes to achieve a tactical, competitive advantage. The tuning or construction occurs during the projects identified in the business architecture phase. The core business process approach is an important modeling technique you will need to build the SOA.

The Role of the Core Business Process

Corporate leadership measures, oversees, and controls the top-level processes. The structure of core processes parallels management structures. Executives monitor the top-level processes while managers measure and control at the subprocess level.

Therefore, a process-oriented approach with BPM simplifies business activity monitoring. This is because BPM tools store and manage the business forms attached to processes at each level. In the Sumter Rents example, we will be able to answer larger scale questions, such as what is the number of bulldozers in a customer assignment, in maintenance, at the store, and others. Similarly, a mortgage company oversees their loan process—how many loans are in data gathering, customer credit checks, or pre- and post-settlement? How long are these processes taking?

You should involve every level of the enterprise in developing the core business process. To develop the processes for Sumter Rents, we use interviewing and research techniques to detail the CBP. Executives are involved in the project start, division managers communicate concerns, and equipment managers in the retail store tell the rest of the story.

To build a CBP, we start with activities—starts, stops, data flows, and subprocesses. This depends on your style, because when you develop CBP, you should get the building blocks right before you put much detail into them.

We developed a logical subprocess model to improve the equipment and customer processes. We used messaging and event techniques to create a process that is independent of the external systems processing the transaction. Imagine going from a Web screen to a cell phone for ordering.

Once you define and detail the core processes, you will set up each ERP—or legacy stovepipe—as a separate service. As we climb above the CBPs, we want to break out the business units in a manner that can be outsourced or insourced. For instance, in the business processes in Figure 3.4, the project team has set up SAP as a subprocess call. Now, Sumter Rents might decide to outsource or replace the SAP application.

FLOW CONTROL ELEMENTS FOR THE CBP

The semantics of our requirement suggest what BPMN should be placed on the process diagram. To build a process orchestration, you match the scenarios of the process needs with a combination of BPMN models. BPMN tools compose a single document for each of the processes.

It is useful to understand what BPMN does and how you use it to manage your processes. BPMN orchestrates services and applications by bridging with Web services. In the past, systems did this orchestration with hardwired computer programs and systems utilities. BPMN concentrates all of this logic for building a composite application so that your application is easy to change. Again, because your team does not have to write these programs, they will spend fewer hours coding.

Setting up Business Rules Within the Business Processes

BPMN often uses Web services to call subprocesses, business rules, and interfaces to external systems. BPMN creates BPEL. Before we look at some BPMN/BPEL, it is important to understand the Web Services Description Language (WSDL). As I mentioned in the introductory chapter, Web services create the late bindings for business rules services. Common characteristics of Web services are:

- Self-contained, self-describing, modular applications that are published, found, and invoked across the Web
- Software modules that describe a collection of operations that are network-accessible through standardized XML messaging
- Loosely coupled software components that interact with one another dynamically through standard Internet technologies

This means that there is no other code in the business process other than the data structure that is needed to invoke the Web service.

An XML WSDL specifies the Web service. The major parts of the WSDL are:

- Types: data that defines the data types used in messages
- Messages: defines the data parts of a communication
- Port Types: defines the exposed operations (similar to a function call in programming languages). Usually there is an input, an output, and a default port type
- Bindings: defines the communication protocols
- Ports: specifies a port address on the Web server for a binding
- Services: collects related ports

Because the Web service needs to pass information into a type or data structure, there is some inherent dependency. If you need to change the record attributes of a business rule, you will need to change the business process. In the next chapter, I will describe how a Web service executes a business rule.

Business Process Modeling and BPMN

Here are some of the basic BPMN choices and the BPEL that supports it. You can get a comprehensive specification for BPMN-BPEL at *www.omg.org*. Although a comprehensive list of BPEL tags is beyond the scope of this book, I hope to show the relationship between the modeling choices, the modeling symbols, and the BPEL that it creates.

Choice/Switch. This is a conditional switch among several choices depending on the process path. The effect of choice and switch are similar. The Choice tag equals an *If … Then … Else* predicate in procedural languages. The Switch tag equals *Case* or *Switch* instructions.

In the BPMN, these tags are shown as a series of paths and activities between the (◇) and the (⊕). The switch evaluates the conditions and selects the activity path associated with the event. For example, the BPEL for the first choice in the equipment process is

```
<<switch name="Inspection"
<case condition="Accept"
<sequence>
<invoke name="Add to SAP"
partner = '…'
inputContainer = equipmentEntity
outputContainer=equipmentEntity
```

```
</invoke>
</sequence>
</case>
<otherwise>
<sequence>
<invoke name="Return to MFR" partner = '...'
</invoke>
<terminate name="Terminate"
</terminate>
</sequence>
</otherwise>
</switch>
```

This choice is from the left side of Figure 3.3. In the BPMN, the Switch tag tells the process engine to evaluate whether or not the equipment has passed the inspection. The Name tag in BPEL is the text that is associated with the diagram.

The Sequence tag defines a series of activities to do. If the program runs an activity as a Web service, or as a separate program, BPEL specifies this with the Invoke tag. The *partner* is a reference to the program or Web service that is used to process the information. The input and output containers are arguments for the program or Web service. The partners and containers are defined at the beginning of the BPMN document. The Terminate tag is shown as a (⊙) on the process diagram.

While. The While activity executes an activity path based on the truth value of a condition. There is an example of a while loop in Figure 3.3. The equipment process uses a while activity to move equipment from the retail store to the customer and to maintenance. Within the process is an activity that waits for a message queue for the equipment. For each message, there is a case that moves the equipment between the retail store, maintenance, or the customer. The idealized BPEL for this is

```
while name="While Inventory"
<sequence>
<invoke name="EquipmentState"
partner="MessagingDestination"
portType="MessageQueue"
```

```
operation="receiveWait"
inputContainer="receiveWait.Input"
outputContainer="receiveWait.Output"
 </invoke>
<switch Name ="Decision"
<case receiveWait.Output.text="SOLD">
<sequence>
<empty name="Empty"
</sequence>
</case>
 <case receiveWait.Output.text ="RetailStore">
<sequence> <invoke name="CheckIntoStore"
… -These ellipsis denote the sub process WSDL's
 </invoke>
</sequence>
 </case>
<case receiveWait.Output.text ="AssignCustomer">
<sequence>
<invoke name="Lease2Customer"
… WSDL
</invoke>
</sequence>
 </case>
 <case receiveWait.Output.text ="Maintenance">
<sequence>
<invoke name="CheckMain"
… WSDL
</invoke>
 </sequence>
</case>
</switch>
</sequence>
</while>
```

There is a case within the while loop that moves the equipment between the customer, the retail store, and maintenance. As well as the Case and While tags, there are many other important BPMN constructions, including

- **Spawn.** The Spawn tag signals the BPEL engine to run the activities in the branches in parallel. For instance, if process A and process B can be run in parallel, then the BPMN would be

```
<sequence>
<spawn name="process A" partner = '...' inputContainer = processAEntity
outputContainer=processAEntity>
 <spawn name="process B" partner = '...'
inputContainer = processBEntity
outputContainer=processBEntity>
</sequence>
```

- **Exceptions.** Business processes raise exceptions with the Exception tag. BPMN denotes exceptions with a ( ). The Throw tag raises the exception. If a switch detects an abnormal condition, then it executes a sequence of activities to recover gracefully from the exception. In this example, BPEL sets up a fault handler, *invalidData*, at the top of the document:

```
<faultHandlers >
<catch faultName="tns:invalidData"
<sequence>
<invoke name="Cleanup"
</sequence>
</catch>
</faultHandlers>
```

In the body of the BPEL, a case block may throw the exception with the Throw tag:

```
<case sbynpx:lineLabel="Case 1">
<sequence>
<throw name="Throw"
```

faultName="tns:invalidData"
</throw>
</sequence>
</case>

- **Schedules/Waits.** Business processes use the Schedule tag ahead of a sequence of activities. The attributes of the schedule are controllable by the business process. BPMN denotes schedules with a (⊚).

The point of this exercise is to show that BPEL gives you a lot of process control in an XML document. The BPEL engine uses the XML file to configure the process. Modeling notation simplifies changes to the BPMN specification. In addition, BPMN is straightforward enough for nontechnical people to use. So, in theory, nontechnical personnel specify much of the process.

TYPICAL PATTERNS FOR BUSINESS RULES IN PROCESSES

Because rules are changed with business rules software, a rule positioned for change makes the entire system more powerful. Managers might tighten a policy. Information managers might reduce the requirements for data. Service manager rules address a customer's special needs. Figure 3.9 shows a typical pattern for a business rules Web service.

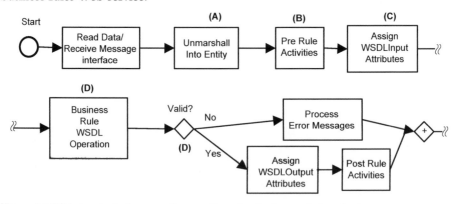

Figure 3.9 This is a typical pattern for a confirmation business rule in a business process.

Again, the figure shows a single part of a business process broken into two parts. The (⅔) symbol stands for a continuation of the process from the upper right-hand side. If you are not familiar with business processes, the flows contain the attributes of the entities that we have described. The steps of the process are as follows:

- At the start, the process unmarshals data into the interface entity (A)
- Intervening activities may take place with the data (B)
- Activities in the process map and assign input/output attributes for the WSDL operation (C)
- The process runs the activity that invokes the Web service. It uses an operation the designer has selected from the WSDL (D)

If the WSDL interface status = error E, we then process the error for the business rule, otherwise we continue along the other path (this assumes the business rule directly returns error messages).

Business rules assign data to the object entity, and a CRM business rule returns a list of customer needed (or preferred) objects. A contract order rule looks at the contract number and date to look up the terms and conditions of the contract.

INTERFACES FOR THE SYSTEMS INVOLVED

After they have detailed the CBP, the project team should design the interfaces. They are always mindful of the needs of users. The application should not require users to enter interface data that does not reflect a business need. Therefore, system designers should hide (or abstract) these details away from the users to the greatest extent possible. Remember that the BPM/BR should link your current networks, business systems, and applications together into a single, seamless information system—the *composite application.*

During the business process modeling phase, we developed the business's needs for a core business process. Independent of this process is the properties that the services must control to interface with different systems, including transportation, engineering, supply chain, and accounting systems.

Once there is a clear understanding of the interface's needs, then the design team maps business forms or entity data to the needs of the external systems. This suggests that they should develop a series of process activities that map the attributes of the business forms to the interfaces for the systems.

Accounting Codes. In the Sumter Rents example, we have created models of the customer and the equipment processes. The models suggest different integration scenarios that the production system must support. What is missing is a way to convert this data into data that the SAP accounting system uses. The design team should create maps that assign the proper transaction codes to each of these transactions.

Other Codes. Applications such as SAP or Oracle Financials use specific metadata set-ups for your organization's data. For instance, you might have several designators for order numbers or responsible organizations. The ERP will populate columns in the database that have been labeled as placeholders. When the business process runs the interface, this information will be useful to the users of the ERP.

There are tools for developing these mappings, such as SAP's Integration Builder. Integration Builder stores interface descriptions in a repository so that the business process can reference them. The Integration Builder publishes the interface as a Web service.

It is my experience that integration teams often need to do work inward, from both sides. New and improved processes change the way an ERP is set up, and the abilities of the ERP will affect the interface processes.

Steps for Interface Success

The Sumter design team uses a four-step strategy to develop the system interfaces:

1. Develop test cases for each of the scenarios for equipment maintenance and customer billing. For instance, for a selection of equipment use *post a recall*, *test a seasonal recall*, and *test usage hour maintenance*. The design team first tests the scenarios using SAP PM screens and reports.

2. Use SAP Interface Builder to create a Web service. Create a simple business process to read a file, and then post the scenarios into the Web service.

3. Add messaging to another business process. Convert the contents of the message to the data in the first scenario. Review the details of the mapping before a full integration. The design team may elect to use the business rules approach to perform some of the mapping.

4. Complete the integration. The team does not try to move data all the way through until they have both sides working.

It may not be possible to test every case. For example, there is a wide range of maintenance schedules. The steps above were designed to corroborate that interface processes work—assuring that the data gets to the process—before they are added to the core process.

In summary, you will want to test your examples in the test instance using a simple interface. It is easier to work with a flat file of the scenarios, loading them into the interface subprocesses, before you do this with a more involved messaging strategy.

Working with an ERP interface can be tedious and difficult. Without some experience on your team, it is risky to try this work. The software industry, however, is simplifying the chore of building interfaces. BPMN suites provide standard interfaces for many ERP systems. These are known as adapters. Adapters reduce the time, cost, complexity, and skills needed to integrate the core business process. The software industry offers a comprehensive set of adapters, and they work seamlessly with many BPM environments.

CONNECTING TO EXTERNAL PARTNERS

When you connect your organization to external partners, your team will use open protocols, such as EDI and B2B business protocols. They will also need to consider *enveloping protocols* that involve exchanging transactions in a secure way and assuring that the intended recipient is the actual recipient. BPM tools support existing standard protocols, with prebuilt business protocol pipelines. They also provide the tools and framework to create and adopt new protocols and to build custom pipelines.

A BPM suite will provide validation, logging, and reporting powers so that you add process steps and business rules, tailoring them to address the particular needs of each eBusiness challenge. Trading partners might exchange information with Collaboration Protocol Agreements (CPAs), which are described at *www.ebxml.org*. Otherwise, you may want to build trading partner profiles manually. Each trading partner profile should be identified by a unique ID determined by the enterprise. Delivery channels for acknowledgments, compression, industry-standard encryption and decryption, and nonrepudiation should be configured.

At run-time, the business process tracks all steps, from the first receipt of the message, to final delivery to the trading partner. You will need tools for recovering and filtering tracked message and envelope information.

THE COMPLETE BUSINESS PROCESS MODEL

To complete a business process, the team details the diagram with the necessary scheduling, exceptions, and structures of the messages. The purpose of the details is to erect a more complete process model. The business processes should act on all the messages, including the system failures. In the real world, business processes are more complex than the first draft:

- The process should handle every possible exception; there are two types of these—business rules exceptions and system exceptions

- The process should *compensate* for transactions that fail to complete. In a compensation, the process cleans up or backs out records from ERPs
- Prerequisite processes must complete, and there could be *delay* actions noted on the diagram

Business processes usually receive a message and translate that message into yet another message that is understood by the next part of the process. Depending on the BPM tool that you are using, the team will need to add implementation code to the diagram for this purpose.

You can model BPs with advanced abilities that suspend processing, or communicate with disconnected, mobile processes. These powers yield opportunities for the enterprise to fine-tune their most complicated practices. They are also positioned to add new technology, such as RFID.

Timing is a new type of input in BI analysis. An analysis of this data provides places where the business can improve its processes. One improvement might be the removal of unnecessary roadblocks by rewriting hardwired processes and creating even looser coupling for flexibility.

Scheduling

BPM suites should provide integrated scheduling and control solutions for all business processes. Most suites have a process control tool that centralizes all procedural business and data processing needs into a simple, consistent, easy-to-administer application. It should support processes in a way that nontechnical personnel can control them.

The business process should be as automatic as possible. There are still many factors that can change schedules. Personnel work during limited hours. Critical data might be posted at a date and time that changes. The manager and business administrators understand the schedules and flow of the business better than the systems administrator or database administrator. Often, these schedules are fluid and changing, and the BPM environment should reduce your dependency upon technical personnel. A schedule editor should be available for the design group to use daily. The manager is freed from going through technical layers to control his or her systems.

Compensations and Exceptions

Certification that all sequences of activities actually complete and are orderly is a key goal of aggregating business processes and Web services. Because transactions in a business process approach might require long periods of time to run through to completion, traditional mechanisms for doing this are not always applicable.

Your processes must continue to run despite unpredictable circumstances. The idea of the LRT relies on groupings of smaller transactions. Therefore, your process will need to be able to undo the effects of a process that fails to complete.

The process design team should design the fault handlers to deal with exceptions during normal processing. They design compensation handlers that reverse the effect of a finished unit of work in a business process. The process invokes the compensation when the normal work of the process is finished. This cleans up the process for the compensation handler to start its reversal activity. The business process starts the compensation handlers by the fault handler of an enclosing scope. The block of activities decides which compensations to process. It also decides in what order to roll back partial work if there is a failure.

A modern business process environment should report to systems administrators when exceptional processes exceptions occur. The process should be able to recover and restart. Systems monitors should be able to view errors and restore the process to its original state. I will discuss exception handling in greater detail in the systems administration chapter of this book.

TESTING THE BUSINESS PROCESS MODEL

Even if the project team needs to work on business rules, they should unit test the processes that they have developed. Testing helps detect and diagnose performance problems before the team finishes the entire project. If there are incomplete business rules, the project members might hand-code sample business rules into dummy subprocesses.

If the team spends time testing these early prototypes, they will create the final product more thoroughly and in less time. They will also be able to catch more defects and release better projects. The other benefit to this early testing is that nontechnical business analysts quickly build and document test cases. This will cut testing time. Furthermore, test documentation and test automation get combined into one formal effort.

Process performance is always a big concern of all the participants in the project. In the Sumter Rents example, there will be thousands of equipment processes running on the server. The Sumter Rents enterprise experiences various business peaks. Testing and tuning for these peaks mitigates the risk of poor performance. And like the value of knowing your daily load, understanding your business peaks allows you that much more leverage when it comes time to perform a major functional upgrade or technology refresh.

Because business activities or functional areas have historical information, the data needed for business peaks should be easy to identify. A key to stress testing is to ensure that the team has enough data to do the job of stress testing.

SUMMARY

Sumter's equipment processes should improve the productivity of the team.

Successful companies, such as Sumter Rents, organize and run their business activities in an efficient way. These companies fulfill their core activities on time and with constrained budgets and personnel. To stay competitive in today's markets, however, successful companies must adjust their business activities to the marketplace. They need to have these activities complete quickly with higher quality and lower costs. Because companies aim to improve their processes, they are exploring the benefits and potential competitive advantages of BPM systems. BPM offers improved efficiencies because they improve the scheduling, execution, and management of business activities.

BPM enables *late binding* software architecture. This new technology can enable higher independence among the processes, which is the purpose of SOAs. Therefore, if you build a business process with BPMN, it should be easier to change business processes and the systems that support them. An activity might provide an interface to an application on a server in the technical infrastructure, yet any system that can provide the service could replace it. With a low dependency on the service (that is, the legacy system), the core business process manages the content and timing of the information sent to those systems that provide services.

There are many benefits in using a BPMN approach with the SOA. By breaking a business into a series of discrete core processes, a company might either offer that service to customers or outsource the service to others. At some point, the business process should deal with the documents that become the transactions in the system. This is where controlling the business process with business rules becomes important. For example, a purchase order or requisition against a contract might need multiple confirmations before the system accepts it. Is the requisitioned item part of the contract? Are there any quantities left for delivery? Is this the best contract vehicle for the requisition? The approach that I am describing here suggests that these design questions be captured as an activity in the business process and then detailed in the business rules phase.

Because they control process flow, business rules also create business events. This is the way an evaluation of a business rule sets business processes in motion. Typical events may include reviews, approvals, product inspections, laboratory tests, maintenance inspections, and financial penalties.

Here are the bullet points of this chapter:

- In the BPM, the design team develops the core business process from interviews and research
- Core business processes perform independently of the systems that provide services to them. The core process should also be reasonably independent of the data entry methods

- All business processes contain flow control elements that orchestrate the process
- Business rules set the parameters that affect flow control in the business process
- As well as enforcing stated policies, you discover powerful control of business processes by examining the flow of the process. Deciding when to take a path within a business process is a good place for a business rule
- BPMN produces BPEL. BPEL is a standard that is utilized by any BPEL engine
- BPMN has a simple and powerful syntax
- Interfaces should be designed after the core business process is designed
- The complete business process handles exceptions and allows transaction to be rolled back with compensations

CHAPTER FOUR: BUSINESS RULES

Business rules make decisions using current information and guidelines. Organizations might change their guidelines, yet rarely will they change the subject of the rule or policy. Predictably, Sumter Rents will always have policies on customer credit, equipment maintenance, and working inventory. What will change are the specifics of the rules—the discount ranges and whom they award them to, or the flexibility of changes in maintenance schedules.

Business rules software manages the rules. For instance, with business rules, Sumter Rents creates discount incentives on equipment in an off-season by updating data in the software. BR develops these rules to incorporate new conditions, lessons learned, and other changes that are then introduced through the software.

As I mentioned earlier, you should isolate your corporate business rules according to core business process needs. Interfaces and adapters use information processing rules to map process data. The business process work that we have done for the Sumter Rents project has identified decision areas for maintenance and customer ordering, and information processing rules for SAP. Classic business rule examples could be a credit-worthy customer or an active contract. These areas should control or constrain business activities across the organization.

The rules team will develop the technical details of business rules that follow what I call the four C's: Classify, Calculate, Compare, and Control. Each step of the BR develops these.

To discover business rules, you should start by building a library of the basic terms of the business. After you develop the basic terms, you then discover special types of these terms from the goals of the business rule. With this library of business terms, your efforts have positioned you to create rules that control business decision areas. You manage this information in a business rules repository. In this chapter, we will develop some business rules for the decision areas in the Sumter Rents project.

S umter's process design team has developed solid prototypes to support equipment maintenance and customer service projects. As a next step in supporting the project objectives, the business rules team analyzes the information and conducts interviews to discover the business rules. They develop the policies and constraints of these rules by reviewing documentation, caucusing managers, and holding workshops.

As in BPM, the rules team develops rules with a cross-functional team. Because Sumter headquarters sets equipment policies, and the retail store carries them out, the business rules team canvasses a wide range of viewpoints. Basing an understanding of the current policies through individual, isolated interviews is unwise. The rules team has found that these teams are able to expose the real rules and produce great insight and reality into the policies.

Divining the line between management and technical terms is not an easy task because not all business terms are nontechnical. Business managers often speak in jargon that is either technical or nearly technical out of a necessity to discuss large business processes in meaningful shorthand. Business rules must be able to use these terms to dissect the policies, objectives, and constraints into technical specifications.

In a business rules approach, the team learns the semantics of a language for specification. The language connects terms and ideas to technical data in the BRR. The project team will need to perform technical steps. Business members, however, specify the key parts of the ideas.

The team confirms the rules with an analytical process that is provided by the tools of the business rules. This analysis should identify incongruence in the logic of the rules, such as unresolved paths, redundant values assigned across the same rule set, and unresolved terms. The analysts develop the business rules through a process of defining terms—then by connecting records, computations, and constraints to these terms. They do this with an understanding of the controls that the process will need. Using a formal statement, rules are entered into the business rules repository. Next, the repository exposes the rules as a Web service. The business rules team is also responsible for analyzing rule sets for consistency and completeness.

So, there are two groups of steps in this activity—gaining the understanding needed to create the business rules, and the act of creating the business rules. In the next section, I am going to focus on what the analyst does to understand the business rules.

SUMTER BUSINESS RULES

During the BPM activity, the team identified places in the flow that would benefit from a business rules approach. In all, the process team identified three decision areas that need business rules analysis. These are

- Policies for retrieving equipment from customers when maintenance is called for

- Rules for validating the equipment inspection data before they are sent to SAP PM

- Assigning the proper discount to a customer's order

In addition to these business activities, there are data processing areas that benefit from the business rules approach; such as converting customer order process data into SAP iDOC. Moreover, Sumter Rents wants to target its most profitable customers for loyalty programs. To do this, the company needs to know more about its customers. It needs to broadcast this information to the company's marketers and customer service representatives.

Policies and Constraints (Offering and Negotiations)

Most experts consider business rules to be a formal way of connecting the enterprise's policies and constraints to information systems. A policy is a plan, or course of action, that is intended to influence and cause decisions, actions, and other matters. Therefore, policies are designed to insure that organizations operate within guidelines in a healthful, nurturing and safe way. A constraint restricts, limits, or regulates—a check. Operating in constraints prevents errors and mistakes. The rules we have identified for Sumter Rents' information systems are examples of corporate policies and constraints. Sumter insures their investment in equipment with their automated equipment maintenance policies. Sumter also aims to raise customer loyalty through their policies. Thus, business rules formalize the critical information processing aspects of an enterprise's business model.

An *offering* is a type of policy that is interesting to the marketing team. Part of CRM develops sales campaigns, or offerings, which raise a business's *wallet share* of a customer. A campaign may be a temporary circumstance targeted to a particular customer—during a business process, a business rule could suggest products that might appeal to that customer. CRM models are well-served by the business rule concept.

A negotiation is another type of policy that is designed to secure the best value for purchases from trading partners. The organization develops business rules for getting the best price for a purchase from a business process. They might use business rules to make offers and counter offers.

Business rules help organizations comply with government regulations. Environmental agencies limit pollution that is emitted into the air and water. When these values are exceeded, the enterprise must produce timely reports. This is another area where a business might benefit from a business rules approach.

Obviously, business rules are intimately involved in the way organizations conduct business, and finance their operations. Business rules protect assets by guarding the way they are managed.

The Four C's

If policy is similar to a computer program, then a business rule is a block of code or a procedure that supports the policy. A business rule is a pro forma specification of a part of a policy or constraint's requirement. The action of the business rule is to define what a business does with the data.

Every business rule does what I call *the Four C's*. Each business rule should classify, calculate, compare, and control. They

- **Classify** the type, the division, or the sort. Sumter has at least two types of customers—the preferred customer and the ordinary customer. Sumter has many different maintenance types—seasonal maintenance, winterizing, periodic, lubricate every 400 hours, and manufacturer recall. A concise business rule will start by filtering what it is decided

- **Calculate**, compute formulas, look up data and statistics, and transform and assign values. Constraints are often numerical. How long has the customer leased the equipment? How much of the credit have we extended to the customer? I have included queries and transformations in the computations. A transformation rule converts input values into useful data

- **Compare** the calculation to the redline. The redline is a key value that must be reached, or not exceeded, or within a specified range

- **Control** what is true or valid, correct or mistaken, and the messages that go with them. Policies are often qualitative—companies reward preferred customers and good employees

With all these parts, the business rules approach develops decisions. I am going to describe how Sumter's team developed the rules needed to finish the business processes.

Of all the C's, the most critical parts of a business rule are the redlines and thresholds of Compare. These are the turning points of the decision. If the value of a calculation is above, below, or within a threshold, then the rule accepts or rejects. Sometimes the threshold is a list. Imagine a status flag that stands for a failed or broken item. There might be several of these that managers change when there is a change in policies.

The business rules approach is a powerful way to control critical details of information processing. In our conversations about Sumter Rents, we will define these controls through the Four C's.

Using the Business Rules Software

The business rules team should use software to manage business rules. Examples are Fair Isaac, Corticon, and iLog. These products allow you to enter the business rules so the rules engine unambiguously translates them into instruction steps. Most of these products can expose the rules to business processes as a Web service.

The power of using this software is in the ease that businesses change their policies and constraints. Usually, the business rules software can immediately carry out changes to the processes that use them. Alternatively, business rules might have effective dates that are set.

A PROCESS FOR THE BUSINESS RULES APPROACH

In my experience, business rules change more frequently than processes. Business rules analysis, therefore, is not always a subsequent activity to business process modeling. Rules should be independent of individual processes. A project might involve improving or developing new business rules. As we described, process modeling invokes business rules when it arbitrates the message's content that is passed among flows among activities.

A business process for the business rules approach is presented in Figure 4.1.

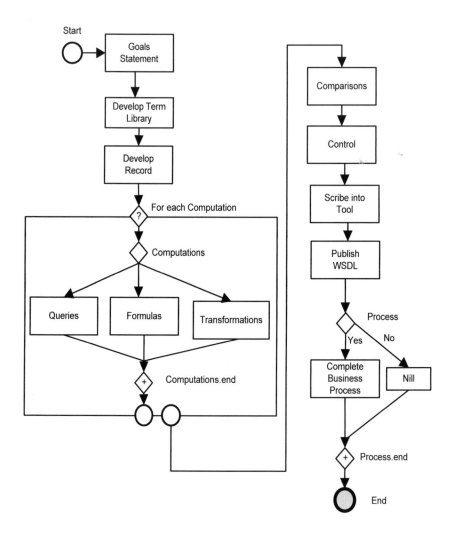

Figure 4.1 A process for developing business rules.

The process applies to each business rule in the project. The workshop's first activity is to agree upon a definitive goal statement for each of the four business rules. The goal must define the outcome of the rule—if it succeeds or fails. The language of the rule suggests the data, the computations, control, and outcome.

Business Rules Activities

The business rules approach is a new design method that is understandable by the manager as well as the technologist. Business managers, executives, and accountants use rules to set the policies and constraints. In a project, business rules carry out the goals that the team set up for each subject area. For instance, a goal might be to limit new product orders to the customer's credit limit. The rules must classify the customer's credit limit, calculate new and old orders, compare the number with the credit limit, then control the ordering process. The redline in this business case is the credit limit.

Business rules use the values of the data in a business form (requisition, reservation) as a basis for each decision. The goal of the business rules is to suggest the needed information. Rules assign meaning to the values of a business form entry. The business rules software needs a dictionary of terms to do this, but I'll discuss that next. In the Sumter Rents project, the two business forms we are working with are the Customer Folio and the Equipment Maintenance Work Order. Business rules use the values from the fields in these forms. These fields are known as *parameters*. Figure 4.2 presents the work order form that is produced by SAP PM. The form is either printed out or emailed to the equipment manager for the store.

Throughout the business rule design phase, the teams develop a dictionary of terms, or parameters, for each rule. These terms signal the flavors of things—a code value for a preferred customer, a delivery mode for a truck, or even numeric data such as ranges and limits.

With the dictionary of terms, the business rules team assembles data records for the business rules to use. In transformations, business rules might look up referential data to assign values to the fields. Many business rules make their decisions on values in more than one field. These records complete the information needs of the rules.

Optionally, the team might decide to develop a fact diagram, or concept diagram, to assess the business goals and the computations needed in processing the data records. For example, utilities that are powered by database queries are needed to bring back supplemental or referential data, or to add or count the values of events.

I consider queries and transformations of data to be types of computation. Computations assign data to records. For instance, in the customer ordering application, the rule must return the customer's discount value to the business process. Computations might include formulas, selections of data such as the maximum or minimum value, or statistical trends.

Sumter Rents Maintenance Work Order

Maintenance Order:MN00Z0	Equipment Id:98034

Model/Serial Number: CAT D6H

Assigned Store:Huntsville	Prn Date: 08/15/2006

Schedule date: 08/19/2006

Odometer Reading(hr):3416

Work Items:
1. 1600 Hr Lubrication, see manual: D6H, 1998, pg 134
2.
3.
4.

Work location:

Completed:

Figure 4.2 Business processes work with virtual business forms. For instance, the maintenance process works with this form.

Sometimes computations within a business rule are the basis for facts in BI. The building blocks for a data warehouse include basic retail queries such as which items were sold, to whom they were sold, and when they were sold. Guidelines and policies might affect this information. In a BI application, business managers review performance indicators that the data warehouse publishes using business rules. Business rules software will state a rule as a predicate. A predicate (*if … then …*) consists of a guard and an outcome. A guard is the Boolean term after the *if*. In the next step of the business rules approach, the team defines the guard of the predicate. This is what I call the comparison part of the business rules approach. Examples might include: *If a customer's credit limit is greater than x* or *If the number of unacceptable items is greater than y*, etc. In the control activity, the business rules team decides what the outcome of the predicate will be based on simple Boolean success or failure. The business rules software publishes the rule as a Web service as described by WSDL.

The final step for the rules method is to incorporate the Web service into the business process. The process team reads the Web service into the business process suite. The WSDL specifies the data that will interact with the business process. The business process invokes an operation in the service. For instance, we decided that business rules were needed to verify the odometer reading on the customer check-in form. When we have published these rules, we will add them to the processes we developed in the last chapter. The process should handle the success or failure of the business rule.

The business rule is an expression of an enterprise's policies or constraints. The business rules approach allows a flexible fine-tuning of the tactics that a competitive organization needs. My approach to business rules is to break the idea into predicate constraints, terms, and computations. Predicate constraints are the *if... then ... else* clauses of the language. Designers use the terms to create collections of data, or records. The rule also uses the data terms to perform calculations, including equations and queries. Business rules use each of these data structures to perform their computations.

The information in the business rules schema creates two critical elements: the metadata and the Web service specification, which gets used in the business process. The diagram shows that the *Rules WSDL* Web service is a virtual doorway to the business rule engine. The doorway passes information back and forth between the process and the engine via the input and output messages created by the business rule. When the service evaluates the business rule, the engine runs the computations and subsequent steps. If the Web service is like a doorway, then the binding service is the pathway for the information.

In the last chapter, we described how the design team found out where to place business rules in the process. The first parts of the BPEL define the services that the partners provide. One of those partners is a business rules service. When you connect the business process with the rules service, the BPM software will need the business rules WSDL to create the service specification. Most BPMN software will incorporate every port and operation in the description. The rule in the business process uses only one port. When it is time to run a business rule, the business process engine prepares an input message and sends it to an operation. The service returns an output message.

Business Rules Concepts

I have depicted the concepts that are carried out in the business rule process in Figure 4.3.

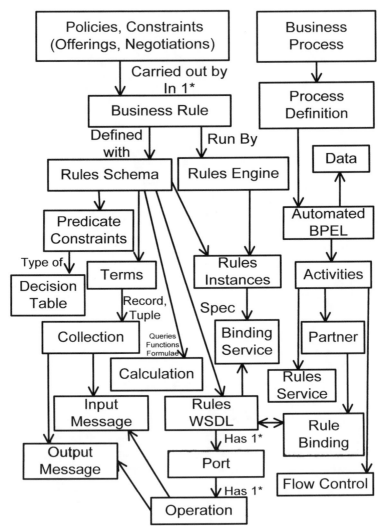

Figure 4.3 This concept schema depicts the things that compose the business rule and its relationship to the business process.

EQUIPMENT MAINTENANCE FOR SUMTER RENTS

Sumter's equipment managers must keep the customers and their management happy.

Equipment is Sumter's largest capital investment. Proper maintenance, while a daunting task, is critical to the preservation of that investment. Scheduled maintenance might come due while a piece of equipment is out on rental. Fetching equipment from customers can be harmful to the productivity of both Sumter and the customer, so Sumter needs to put in place rigorous policies regarding how this issue is handled. If Sumter Rents must recall the equipment, then it should replace the equipment with an equivalent item. There might, therefore, be two rules variations—a rule for when to exchange the equipment and a rule for when to bring back the equipment.

Sometimes manufacturers discover safety defects in their products, and issue recall notices to customers. In this case, Sumter immediately brings back or repairs the equipment. If equivalent equipment is available, then the customer is provided with a replacement.

Most of Sumter Rents' heavy equipment must undergo full lubrication every 400 to 600 hours of operation, or every 6 months. Heavily used equipment needs frequent service, and preferred customers often lease this equipment for periods of time that exceed this limit.

When equipment is returned from a customer, the equipment manager enters the operation hours into an equipment return form. It is easy to incorrectly enter the reading, and this might miscue the schedule in SAP PM. Until the equipment's onboard computer data are available through RFID, Sumter will need to develop a logical check for data. For instance, if the engine hours are less than preceding recorded hours, then the odometer reading is wrong.

Maintenance Goals

The business rules team holds meetings and workshops to develop the rules for the maintenance business process. The cross-functional team includes the top manager of equipment, a director of customer quality, and equipment managers from the retail stores. They reach a consensus on the policies for maintaining the customer-assigned equipment. They agree on a goal of how to decide when to bring back the equipment from the customer in the case of scheduled maintenance or manufacturer recall. The rules team states the goals as follows:

- If equipment is scheduled for maintenance and the reason is not a manufacturer recall, and the customers lease is greater than a set period (let's call the period between the scheduled maintenance and the tolerance for replacement, *replacement time tolerance*), and there is replacement equipment available, then the equipment can be brought back from the customer and replaced with an equivalent piece of equipment

- If equipment is scheduled for maintenance and the maintenance is not a manufacturer safety recall, and the customer's lease is greater than another set period (let's call the period between the scheduled maintenance and the greatest time for delay in maintenance, *greatest time tolerance*), and there is no replacement equipment available, then the equipment can be brought back from the customer, repaired, and returned
- If the equipment is scheduled for maintenance, and the maintenance is a safety recall, then the equipment can be brought back. If equivalent equipment is available, then the equipment can be replaced

I suggest that every goal should be stated as a predicate (*if … then … else*). The texts *Business Rules Applied*, by Halle, or *The Business Rules and Information Systems*, by Morgan, present many different approaches to defining business rules. You might, however, also use a form that more specifically suits your needs. Your rules should be concise and nontechnical. Note that the three goals are separate and their execution is not dependent on order.

Usually, Sumter should have replacement equipment for the customer. Some of the equipment, however, might be rare or in high demand, and Sumter might not have an available replacement.

We see that there are two different (time) redlines that would cause the equipment manager to bring back the equipment. The equipment maintenance subprocess in Chapter 3 will continue to check these times until the equipment is returned, or until time has passed one of the threshold values. There are no fixed constants for the time that will cause the business rule to fire an action in the business process. Rather, the time varies with the urgency of the maintenance. For instance, we would not want to return a bulldozer when all that is needed is a small, noncritical task. Ideally, the business should build a decision table for the maintenance to be performed and the associated times. I have presented a decision table in Table 4.1.

Table 4.1 Redline values for the type of maintenance and the allowable schedule slippage. The replacement time is the allowable period that the manager can wait for the return of the equipment when there is an equivalent replacement available for the customer's leased equipment. The maximum time is the greatest time that the manager waits regardless of available equipment.

Maintenance Type	Replacement Time	Maximum Time
Recurring Lubrication	30 Days	50 Days
Manufacturer Recall Minor	60 Days	90 Days
Manufacturer Recall Major-Safety	1 day	1 Day
Other	60 Days	90 Days

Business rules software allows managers to change these times and add more maintenance types and times. The details of what the business rules must perform are as follows:

- **Maintenance Event Data Elements**: The important data elements for the maintenance business rule include the date of the scheduled maintenance, the current date, the equipment identifier, the equipment maintenance types, and the customer's location. These fields suggest the keys for a logical record for the maintenance business rule

- **Maintenance Event Classification**: The rule classifies the maintenance. There is a separate goal for manufacturer recall

- **Maintenance Event Computations**: There are three computations:

  - The category of maintenance identifies the redline values from the maintenance type decision table

  - The time from the schedule to the current date sets the days from the scheduled maintenance

  - A data query discovers available replacement equipment

- **Maintenance Event Comparison**: The rule compares the redline values against the number of days from the current date

- **Maintenance Event Control**: If the time elapsed has passed the replacement time, return a message that the customer's equipment should be replaced with an equivalent unit. If the time elapsed has passed the maximum time, then return a message for personnel to bring back the equipment at once. In these cases, the value of the business rule should be false or invalid, and error messages should be sent to the process

Some maintenance type codes define a recurring lubrication. In configuring a business rules engine, the analysts either create a function that looks at the list to decide that it is a recurring lubrication, or they create multiple entries in the decision table. These entries would list the technical values for the maintenance type. This, however, would make the decision table more technical and less accessible to managers.

The query that looks for a replacement equipment type would scan the operational data store described in Chapter 3. Customers reserve equipment by category, so data in the customer-relationship process influences this business rule.

When computations are identified with a dictionary term, other business rules reuse these computations and classifications. The business rules repository should allow the analyst to name the computation with a familiar business term. The business rules approach builds a library of these terms. Some business rules approach analysts consider these separate business rules. This finishes the business rule definition for the customer-issued, maintenance event business rule.

Odometer Rules

The business rules design team next turns their focus to the rules for certifying the odometer reading (miles and hours) for equipment whose maintenance schedule calls for a correct value. When the customer returns equipment to a retail store, the rental technician fills out an equipment inspection form. Because the store clerks manually read the odometer, their errors have created miscues in SAP PM. For instance, if a clerk *boxes*, (inverts two numbers) then the number might be an order of magnitude smaller. An invalid entry might cause an incorrect maintenance order.

The team designs this business rule to avert a simple data error by looking at the information in the system's operational data store. They base the rules on a logical examination of the data:

- If the equipment calls for an odometer reading and the odometer reading is less than the preceding reading then the input value is rejected
- If the equipment calls for an hours odometer reading and the odometer reading is greater than 80% of the hours the customer had the equipment, then the input value is rejected. This set of business rules decides when to accept or reject the odometer readings fed to SAP PM to trigger maintenance work orders. You can see that there are no constant redline values for odometer readings. The business rule follows theses steps:

- **Odometer Reading Data Elements**: The important data elements are the equipment identifier, a customer identifier, the equipment type, and the odometer reading.
- **Odometer Reading Classification**: The rule classifies the equipment as calling for an odometer reading. The rule classifies the odometer reading type in hours or miles
- **Odometer Computations**: There are three computations:

  1. The equipment type controls whether the equipment needs an odometer reading.

  2. A query recalls the preceding odometer reading.

  3. A query computes the maximum probable usage hours. Construction crews often use the equipment 20 hours a day, so this maximum time is computed as 20 times the number of days (or fraction).

- **Odometer Reading Comparison**: The input odometer reading is compared with the preceding odometer reading and the maximum probable odometer reading
- **Odometer Reading Control**: If the odometer reading is less than the preceding odometer reading or greater than the maximum probable reading, then it will return a message stating the user has mistaken the odometer reading. In these cases, the value of the business rule should be *false*, or *invalid*. It might be expedient for the rule to provide the earlier odometer reading in the error message

You might connect the odometer rules with the Customer Maintenance Event rule. It seems that when odometer hours drive critical maintenance, there is a gap of information while the customer has the equipment. A suggested improvement would be to estimate the hours of use while a construction contractor has leased the equipment, and then anticipate when the next maintenance should be performed.

The business rule presumes the queries are available for data shown in the concept diagram of Figure 4.4. In the concept diagram, the equipment is assigned to a customer and is the target of a current maintenance work order. The customer maintenance business rule will need to query the work order category. Next, it will need to find out if there is equipment of the same classification available in the store inventory.

Equipment Maintenance Data Concepts

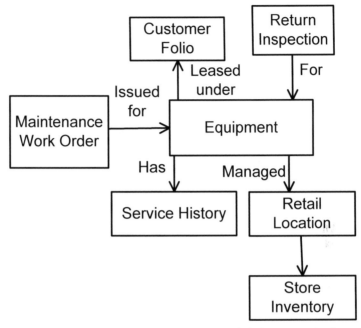

Figure 4.4 This concept schema depicts the data composition of the business rules for customer maintenance returns and the odometer reading.

When the customer returns the equipment, a store clerk finishes a return inspection. The clerk enters the odometer reading as a part of the inspection. The business rule will need to query for the class of odometer (hours or mileage) reading and the preceding odometer reading. When the business process is ready to run this business rule, it should provide the needed data. The customer maintenance business rule will need a simple record type that is expressed in a data type definition, such as

```
<?xml version="1.0" encoding="UTF-8"?>
<!ELEMENT customerMaintenanceRule (EquipmentId, CustomerId)>
<!ELEMENT EquipmentId (#PCDATA)>
<!ELEMENT CustomerId (#PCDATA)>
```

When the business rule is exposed as a Web service, business rules software should create the data type. With the data type definition and business process software, the type is automatically incorporated into the flows.

The equipment identifier will identify its type to the business rule. The rule needs the maintenance type to find the redline value for the time. The process shown in Figure 3.4 in the preceding chapter sends a message stating that the equipment should be maintained. Queries should look up the maintenance tickets and find the maintenance types. The location of the equipment, and the availability of the class of equipment, is developed from the customer identifier.

The odometer business rule will need a simple record type that is expressed in a data type definition, such as

```
<?xml version="1.0" encoding="UTF-8"?>
<!ELEMENT odometerRule (EquipmentId, OdometerReading)>
<!ELEMENT EquipmentId (#PCDATA)>
<!ELEMENT OdometerReading (#PCDATA)>
```

The equipment identifier finds the equipment type and the need for an odometer reading. The preceding odometer reading is also available from the equipment identifier.

These record types are used as input for the WSDL. Later, I will describe how the Web service performs the business rule and how it interacts with the process.

CUSTOMER BUSINESS RULES

Next, the business rules team develops the rules needed for the customer relationship business process. The cross-functional team includes the marketing manager, the manager of customer contracts, and the retail store managers. The team explores two rule sets: a customer discount and a notice system.

Sumter gives preferred customer discounts in various amounts. Sumter also carries out short-term special offerings at different locations and different times. The special offerings are for classes of construction equipment. A class of equipment might be, for example, a 4 ton bulldozer or a 5 cubic yard dump truck. The rules should compute the lowest available discount for the reserved item.

Occasionally, customers might wish to be alerted when a certain equipment type is available for leasing. The rules should limit this notice to those creating a reservation folio. The notice should be removed either after the customer accepts the equipment, or at the customer's direction.

Customer Discount

The goal of the customer discount rule is as follows:

- If the customer is a preferred customer, then find his negotiated discount. If the equipment has special discounts at the location for the stated date, then find the discount. Return the greater of the two values
- If the customer is not a preferred customer and the equipment has special discounts at the location, then find the discount. If there is a discount then return the value

The details of what the business rules must perform are as follows:

- **Customer Discount Data Elements**: The important data elements are the customer identifier, the equipment type, and the equipment location
- **Customer Discount Classification**: The rule classifies the customer as a preferred customer
- Customer Discount Computations: There are two computations:
  1. Using the customer identifier, look up the customer's negotiated discount.
  2. Using the retail store location and the equipment type, look up a discount for the location and the equipment type.
- **Customer Discount Comparison**: Compare and return the greater of the two discounts
- **Customer Discount Control**: The discount will be applied to the estimated bill for the customer's rental folio. The rule should always return a *true* and an assigned discount of zero or greater

This business rule allows the store managers to create short-term rental incentives. During slow periods they may elect to apply a discount to unleased inventory. The managers will need the application to connect to the data that the business rule uses to compute the local discount.

Customer Notification

The goals of the customer notification business rules are as follows:

- If the customer is a preferred customer and the class of equipment for a rental order is not available, and the customer has chosen to get notice of availability, then the notice is turned on.
- If the customer has received the quantity and class of equipment that he requested, then the notice is turned off.

- If the customer requests no further notice, then the notice is turned off.

The details of what the business rules must perform are as follows:

- **Customer Notification Data Elements**: The important data elements are the customer identifier, an acceptance attribute, the class of equipment, and the order number that holds the store location of the equipment and the rental time frame
- **Customer Notification Classification**: The rule classifies the customer as a preferred customer. The rule classifies the acceptance attribute as affirmative
- Customer Notification Computations: There are two computations:
  1. From a query, discover if the store has issued all the items the customer has requested. This query uses the order number
  2. From a query, find out if the class of equipment is available at the location for the rental period. This query uses the equipment identifier
- **Customer Discount Comparison**: Check the availability of equipment in the preferred class, at the specified location for that date
- **Customer Discount Control**: When there is available equipment, notify the customer through the manner requested

The primary users of this notice are customers needing a short-term lease of equipment that is in high demand. To use this feature, they create a reservation for equipment they know is not immediately available. Once other customers return equipment, and the store inspects it, they receive a notice from the retail store that it is available.

The management team considered many ideas in developing this rule. They considered adding a model to the prompting list so the customer could be more specific about the notice. For instance, the customer may want a Caterpillar® versus a Kubota®. Because of the service-oriented approach, this rule should be simple to add later.

Customer Data Concepts

As in the maintenance customer rules, there must be queries that support the needed calculations. Figure 4.5 shows the concepts for this.

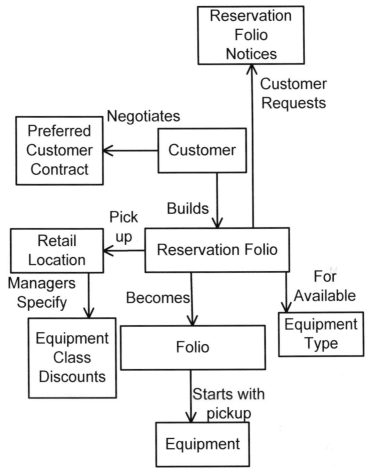

Figure 4.5 The Customer Business Discount rule needs to find the customer's discounts and notify the customer about equipment availability when the reservation is placed.

For the Customer Discount Business rule, the information we need must identify the customer's discount and the equipment class discounts. The customer discount is part of the negotiated contract for a preferred customer. The equipment type discounts are associated with a retail location. The manager offers discounts to lower his excess inventory.

If customers reserve an equipment type that is unavailable, then the reservation folio might report other available equipment. Whether or not the customer uses the feature, the notice should be logged every time a customer requests unavailable equipment. Management uses this information to decide if more equipment is needed at the retail store.

These data ideas identify the input data types for the discount business rules. A data-type definition expresses a simple record type in

```
<?xml version="1.0" encoding="UTF-8"?>
<!ELEMENT customerDiscountRule ( CustomerId, reservationFolioId, discount)>
<!ELEMENT customerDiscountRule (#PCDATA)>
<!ELEMENT reservationFolioId (#PCDATA)>
 <!ELEMENT discount (#PCDATA)>
```

These data concepts also identify the input data types for the notification business rules. A simple record type is expressed in a data type definition:

```
<?xml version="1.0" encoding="UTF-8"?> <!ELEMENT
customerNoticeRule ( CustomerId, reservationFolioId, onOff)>
<!ELEMENT customerDiscountRule (#PCDATA)>
<!ELEMENT reservationFolioId (#PCDATA)> <!ELEMENT onOff (#PCDATA)>
```

These record types will be used in the business processes to connect the business rule to the Web service.

WEB SERVICES FOR BUSINESS RULES

Web services use a client/server model. The business process is an example of a client, and the business rules engine is an example of a Web service server.

Clients of Web services interact with those Web services through port types and operations. A port type is the name of the entry point for the service, like a virtual doorway. Attached to each port type are optional inbound data (input) and optional outbound data (output). Web services support many different port types. These comprise

- *One-Way*: only input
- *Request-Response*: only output
- *Solicit-Response*: input and output
- *Notice*: only output

Business rules should use the *Solicit-Response* port type. The business rule has input (request) and output (reply). Information is input for confirmation. Business rules output provides three types of output: valid or invalid, transformed data, and error messages.

Figure 4.6 explains how the business process runs the business rule in the rules engine as a client to a service-binding server. On the server, the *DiscountRule* port type, has an operation called *Validate*. In the BPEL engine, the process assigns values to the customer identifier and the reservation identifier.

Figure 4.6 The Web service for the customer discount uses the input data to apply the business rule and return the proper discount.

The business rules engine consumes the data and then runs through the computations, comparisons and controls—finally returning values. If no errors occur, the value returned is the customer discount and the *Valid* field set to *true*. If there are errors, for instance the rule could not match a customer identifier with a record, then the *Valid* field is set to *false* and error messages are returned.

The following fragment of the specification details how a WSDL could specify the port and operation for the scenario shown in Figure 4.6.

```
<wsdl:portType name="DiscountRule">
```

```
<wsdl:operation name="validate">
<wsdl:input message="inputCustomerDiscount"/>
<wsdl:output message="outputCustomerDiscountType"/>
</wsdl:operation>
</portType> <wsdl:message name="inputCustomerDiscount">
<wsdl:part name="in0" type="tns2:customerDiscount"/>
</wsdl:message>
<wsdl:message name="inputCustomerDiscount">
<wsdl:part name="in0" type="tns2:customerDiscountout"/>
</wsdl:message>
```

Again, the advantage to the Web service is that you can change the computer program the port and the operation calls while avoiding changes to the client— the business process. Procedural code is inside the business rules engine, working out the details that we designed when we created the business rule.

Architecturally, the business process or application does not encase the business rules. Rather, the Web service treats the business rule like a procedural call from a computer language. This is why Web services and business processes interact well with business rules. The business rules software publishes a rule for, let's say, a customer or employee policy, and many different systems can use that same rule. With the loosely connected architecture described here, a constraint, policy, or computational change often will not affect the process itself. Unless the input record changes, you change underlying computations and reference data with no impact to the Web service.

RULES AND THE BUSINESS OBJECT

In Figure 4.6, the business object puts the business rule into effect. A business object is an object (in this case, the customer discount object) that contains all the attributes, records, and computations that carry out the policy or constraint goals. Sometimes a business object runs a business use case that creates a business transaction, which is a part of the LRT of the business process.

Business rules repositories usually have either an engine or an application generator that use metadata or business rules, respectively, to produce computer code. Either approach enforces the basic constraints, policies, and doctrine of the enterprise. The code creates a bridge or a deductive connection from the business rule to the process.

ADDING BUSINESS RULES TO THE BUSINESS PROCESS

Once the business rules team generates (publishes) the Web service, the business process team adds the rule. Most BPM software has utilities that make this task simple. The BPM software should read the WSDL and create data types for the input and output.

For each of the processes that use a Web service, there are a few extra steps you will need to take. You should map the form attributes of the business process to the input of the service. Your mapping may need some conversions, such as converting numbers to strings and strings to dates. The process team will need to decide what to do if the business rule fails, and what to do with error messages.

In Figure 3.6 in the last chapter, I presented the customer relationship process. The process team might set up the business rule for the customer as a subprocess as follows:

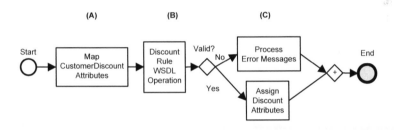

Figure 4.7 The Web service for the customer discount might be implemented as a subprocess.

In Step (A), the process maps the customer identifier and the location identifier to the input for the Web service. In Step (B), the process calls the Web service operation. In Step (C), the process either encounters an error or maps a discount to the output of the service.

SUMMARY OF BUSINESS RULES CONCEPTS

In a BPM/BR project, the business processes are responsible for the flow of data that is fed into the business rules. The business rules activity defines and manages the content of application transactions, collaborative transformations, systems procedures, and other rules. These might include business-to-business processes. Core processes use the business form developed by your organization. You use the business rules approach to map this form to a record needed by the ERP packages. This is called creating a canonical, or basic, form. The details of the exchange of information can be isolated from changes to the ERP package.

Business rules also

- Define measures and dimensions for construction of fact schemas in the data warehouse
- Inspect or report metrics and dimension ranges across aggregated data. This will be covered in the next chapter
- Carry out directed, short-lived special offerings. This is a key feature of CRM. We suggested this in our customer discount rule. Because the BPM/BR positions the application for change, it can carry out short-term product campaigns, time, and availability limitations
- Permit exceptions to hard and soft rules, allow customers and trading partners to bypass procedures and prevent invalid interactions

The process for developing business rules is dependent on the project's nature. Because organizations use the BPM/BR for creating a combination of integrations, operational systems, or data warehouses, each process will be slightly different. For instance, if attributes are to be transformed for an ERP, then business rules are the result of mapping those attributes. If the organization is developing policies for financing customer purchases, then the management team needs to develop these rules in a collaborative way.

Classes of Business Rules

The simplest part of the business rule is the statement of a term. In a business rules project, an early step is to collect all the needed terms. Collectively, terms define singular, high-level ideas. When the analysis changes the term into various flavors and types, they trigger a special subset of business rules.

For instance, a contract might be a term—then a fixed-fee contract becomes a modified term. A customer might be a term—a foreign customer becomes a modified term. Each of these data classifications classifies business rules.

The computations in business rules build on modified terms. For instance, some rules might look up or transform record attributes. A rule might need to query a customer's data from a credit card number. Another rule's query might recall payment terms for an invoice from the contract number. When this happens, these subtypes apply to more business rules.

A business rule controls with redline values such as constraints, and minimum or maximum conditions. Such values invoke other rules or control something in a business process. Control might override prior choices or control decisions based on time durations. Because business rules apply the same way to any process that uses them, they are an excellent way to state and enforce policies.

For instance, a factory order is an *LRT* that affects many different systems. As the business processes runs, business rules act on the cumulative transaction. Business rules work with business forms compared with data models. A business rule jumps from field to field on the business form. The business rule's data hierarchy is like a paper business form over the entities of a data model. A data model contains many different business cases. A business form is a single business case.

Different organizations can call the same idea by different names. In the BPM/BR, we call these *aliases*. They might even have different values mapped across these aliases—applying the policies and constraints of that organization and cutting out the stovepipe disconnection (an important aim of EAI). The rules of the discipline—say, accounting compared with manufacturing—instantiate their own semantically correct version of the rules.

A business rule positions the details of the idea for global changes. Policies are often about the timely reporting of accounting data, process connections, and available resources. If changes result from analysis such as economic analysis, business intelligence, responses to the competitive environment, or government regulations and laws, then the enterprise can easily change the rule.

SUMMARY

The results of the business rules analysis activity are the goals, data dictionary, and entries in the business rules tool. The output is also the connection of the business rules engine with the business process.

BPM tools easily build applications that manage the streams of business forms. They are excellent for managing the *when* and *where* of a business scenario. Processes automatically route data to the correct system. Yet, it is easy to put too much application code in a BPM tool, especially if this code—the stuff we want to specify in business rules—is going to change. Simplistically, I call this the *why* part of the business. For instance, you might develop a complex loan qualification process that calls data from database tables and Web services. If it is constantly changing, then I would suggest that this be one process activity that should call a business rule Web service.

When the BPM/BR team uses a business rules analysis to discover, analyze, and group the business rules, they are supporting a tree-like structure of decisions, policies, and constraints for the business. Examples include the best source for a requisition, or when to salvage a fixed asset. Policies might include who is qualified for a loan. The branches of the tree start with the statement of a term and become more complex as the rule uses the term in records and computations. Business rules specify constraints, or redline values. These are the minimum or maximum conditions for invoking other rules, overriding low-level choices, or deciding the time duration for a condition.

Our goal is to be able to maintain process and procedures separately from the validations of decisions. Business rules sentences are themselves loosely connected to the architecture through the Web interfaces. Structurally, a business rule positions an idea for rapid, global change.

If you intend to create a composite application, then you will probably need composite business rules. Information comes from many sources in the SOA. It is important to set up loose binding among the origins of the validation data needed by the rules. You might use services to separate technical details from reference data or transactions from implementation—you might change the source of the data without changing the business rule and without changing the process.

Business rules are associated with and affect transactional data exchanges and business events. Business rules uniquely specify a corporate use of the business process. In other words, special practices and tactics are put into effect in the business rules.

Here are the bullets that you should take away from this chapter:

- Business rules classify, compute, compare, and control data to direct the flow in a business process
- Business rules can certify the data in the business forms
- When developing your business rules, you should write out the goal of the business rule in simple English
- The goal should suggest the data you need and the computation that should be performed
- The business rules approach builds a dictionary of business terms. These terms include labels for computations
- The business rules software publishes the business rule in terms of a Web service

Clear business rules supported by a robust business process make everyone's life easier.

CHAPTER FIVE: BUSINESS INTELLIGENCE

Effective executive leadership solves problems large and small. With Sumter Rents, suppose a bulldozer lays unused because of the indolence of a few employees. Someone has not ordered a critical spare part. Can you find the little circumstances in your business that adds up to big costs? Are there glitches in the operations and processes that your employees could easily correct?

Looking at the big picture, managers use Business Intelligence (BI) to evaluate the condition or performance of their areas of responsibility with key performance indicators and other metrics. With BI, you create a system that pictures these metrics with a dashboard—speedometers, gauges, and box-and-whisker plots. When a particular measure is out of range, the manager easily drills into the underlying data to discover the issues and the problems.

The dashboard monitors standard productivity measures, such as cost of sales, inventory turnover, and others. With a BPM approach, the dashboard also oversees the efficiency of process execution. A process performs at a particular speed and each step takes time. By combining business metrics and process performance, we arrive at a new understanding—business activity monitoring.

BI can hold data and computations that are in business processes and business rules engines. Managers use BI to identify the rules and processes that contribute to poor (or outstanding) performance.

BI has a role to play in the SOA. Imagine metrics that ferret out poorly performing products at a retail store. With a Web service and a composite application, you could send reports to the managers responsible for the product, suspend shipments from the manufacturer, and alert the purchasing agent. Most BI vendors provide Web service interfaces to their environments that assist in this process.

BI aids executive decisions and business monitoring with data warehousing. Organizations like Sumter Rents oversee their performance with BI. Government and industry increasingly use BI to strengthen their decision processes. Their goal is to understand and identify what factors affect productivity or performance metrics. BI depicts performance with a simple dashboard of thermometers, gauges, speedometers, and other widgets. When the dashboards are driven by current information, BI becomes Business Activity Monitoring (BAM). With the BI approach, a manager is only a few mouse clicks away from the detailed data that powers the dashboard's features.

The BI dashboard insulates users from the complexities of a database. A BI dashboard consists of

- Display controls that depict metrics through a Managed Query Environment (MQE). This allows nontechnical analysts to examine the data behind the metrics. The user can customize the focus of the metrics
- A data warehouse of information that compiles the metrics for the dashboard, and monitors and stores the details of the computations
- An MQE repository that stores queries, details of graphical screens, and report presentations. The repository controls security for users, and groups of users

The promise of the BI environment is that managers will get an expressive representation of the information that models their business. This allows even nontechnical managers to gain insights into complex operational business trends. They will spend a large part of their time analyzing data—fully aware of subtle shifts in the business environment. The BI approach will eclipse the efforts of specialized data analysts. The manager will be able to progressively dissect a metric in a business circumstance. For instance, if a retail store is consistently underperforming in one area, managers use BI to identify this problem and adjust the causes.

To create a BI environment, your team should build an analytical data warehouse for managers and other decision-makers. The outcome of a BI project should be a creative, exploratory tool.

In many enterprises, important decision-making metrics are scattered across a diverse landscape of systems. This is why BPM is a powerful way of gathering this data. Combining data warehousing and BPM provides a method of integrating the disparate stovepipes of information.

The team's earlier effort in business processes and business rules will support the analysis needed for creating BI. Business rules helps to define the dimensions and measures. The trick is to use the analysis of BPM and BPM/BR to provide the information needed to enhance the data schema for the data warehouse.

Hardee's used Business Intelligence to create their successful, albeit over the top, product called the Monster Burger.

STRATEGIC BUSINESS INTELLIGENCE FOR SUMTER RENTS

Sumter Rents' income comes from leasing equipment. Naturally, Sumter's accountants and business managers have developed rental rates for every equipment type in their inventory. As we will see, the important assumption in their rate computation is the number of days the equipment will be leased over the life of the equipment. Eventually, customer rental sales volume is proportional to Sumter's inventory.

Because equipment leasing is Sumter's core business, creating and restocking a quality inventory is a fundamental, budgeted part of this activity. Sumter's customers also enjoy the convenience, safety, and efficiency of the new models.

Unlike automobiles, much of Sumter's aged fleet of bulldozers, cranes, motorized lifts, and other heavy equipment, keeps significant marketplace value. Much of the new equipment funding comes from the capital from the sales of existing inventory. Recently, overseas markets have put upward pressure on the price of used equipment.

In previous years, Sumter has haphazardly sold a portion of the existing inventory. Because there is a high demand for quality used construction equipment, the managers of Sumter aim to plan their sales and new purchases using a BI system. When Sumter buys and sells equipment, it is adjusting its rental inventory. Overall, Sumter managers know they need a more surgical approach. The challenge is to choose the ideal number of units to buy and sell by matching the rental inventory to customer demand.

The BI team meets with the managers from almost every division of Sumter Rents. There were many issues discussed. Among these were

- How do we improve sales projections?
- What is the cost of restocking the leasing capacity?
- How do we avoid selling too much inventory, or selling it too late?

What came from these meetings was a consensus that rental inventory should be better planned. A balance is needed between revenue from used equipment sales, new capital investment, and projected rental sales. The analysis should be a combination of statistics and BI.

The goal is a best fit between inventory and customer demand. To develop projections of customer demand, the BI team will need to assemble, store, and analyze detailed rental sales data. If this information is timely, it will become a powerful analytical and monitoring tool that provides insights into Sumter's performance. Managers will also be able to pay closer attention to the many details and trends of the business.

The *Engineering News Record* publishes regional construction activity indexes that predict construction activity. This is used to predict changes in demand for Sumter's heavy equipment. Sumter managers plan to perform a multivariate regression analysis of their demand against this data.

Sumter Rents aims to develop a preferred customer program to build loyalty with their largest customers. Therefore, if the rental sales information includes customer data, then the BI environment should be able to identify those customers.

A PROCESS FOR BUSINESS INTELLIGENCE IN BPM/BR

Figure 5.1 presents a business process for developing BI for the BPM/BR project.

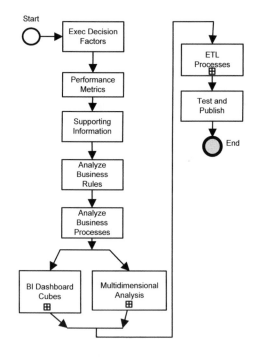

Figure 5.1 This is a basic process for developing BI for the project.

The first step is to develop the factors for executive decisions. How does top management evaluate business activity performance? In general terms, what are the metrics or key performance indicators for the business activity?

To carry out BI, you will need to develop performance metrics that are relevant to the business activity. The project team will need to research and approve a proposed method of computing the metrics. The computations use information the team gathered. At this phase, as a prelude to creating the manager's performance dashboard, the formula will be a specification that data designers use to verify their model.

The next step is to identify the topics, entities, and events that are needed to support the decisions. An entity might be a customer or one unit of equipment. Events are equipment purchase, a customer lease or return, and maintenance. This step is a prelude to loading the data warehouse and performing data analysis.

The BI team will need to explore business rules for the relevant business activity. Business rules define important redline values (limits and constraints) that should be a part of the details that managers see in the queries. Business process software collects time duration data for processes. The team should dissect business processes for performance and other factors that would be useful for the manager's analysis.

The team develops prototypes of the BI dashboard and underlying cubes. At the same time, they develop the multidimensional data structures. Figures 5.2 and 5.3 present these subprocesses.

Metrics and key performance indicators are aggregate measurements of the facts associated with one or more events (orders, sales, or receipts) or financial accounts. In multidimensional analysis, the BI team builds a table layout that the query environment uses to compute the metrics. First, they select a time granularity—or slice of time—for the Extraction, Translation and Load (ETL) process to aggregate the data. For instance, if metrics need monthly data, then ETL condenses daily data into a month format.

Next, the BI team adds dimensions to the facts so that the metrics are computed to various levels of detail. For instance, if a metric is about a retail store, then the team is likely to add higher dimensions of city, state, and sales region. In general, they start with a table layout (DDL) of the tables in the source systems. An analysis of business rules might reveal dimensions that are not obvious by looking at the source data structures alone. Business processes may also have useful timing information about steps.

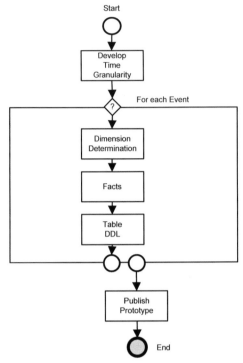

Figure 5.2 This is the multidimensional analysis subprocess.

After the team models the facts, they build a table layout (DDL). This is the physical design of the data structure. They might build a rapid prototype and populate it with sample data. This is useful for the executive dashboard or scorecard development.

When the team builds the dashboard or scorecard, they select a fitting widget for the executive metric. The selection is based on the monitoring imagery you need. Monitoring might include trends, key performance indicators, correlations, thresholds, and others. Examples include the *thermometer* and the *box and whisker*. These might include limits on target values and current values. Widgets may depict a warning symbol that stands for a serious condition that the manager needs to explore. The manager controls the level at which the metric is computed—company wide, sales region, state, and others.

For each of the widgets, the designers design cubes that reveal the data that supports the metric. This is where the user might slice and dice the facts behind the metric. In this process, a user searches for the critical information that reveals underperformance.

In addition to executive metrics, BI environments produce standardized reports. The MQE software pushes reports to decision-makers and managers.

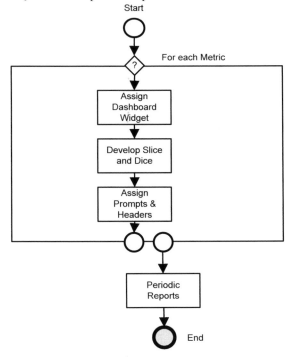

Figure 5.3 This is a process for developing the executive dashboard.

The ETL process populates and updates information in the tables. I have shown this as a subprocess because your design team should do this with a business process (see Chapter 3). If there are several source systems, then you might need to encode common value dimensions. By encoding, I mean the ETL process converts codes and lists into a single standard. This translation is well suited to a business rules approach. Some business process vendors have added ETL abilities to their product suites that automate the process of building data warehouse records from many sources. In the last step of a BI process, the team will certify the result. The executive metrics should be confirmed with data and management review. Finally, the BI system is published for use by decision-makers.

BI and data warehousing has been around for years. Data warehouses are built to spew out mounds of data. What executives and managers need, however, is data in the context of how the business is performing. You should include data that affects the conduct of dealings with a customer or other productive task. Managers are already measuring some of this. If something is underperforming, then this information provides insights.

BI Concepts

BI concepts are included in Figure 5.4.

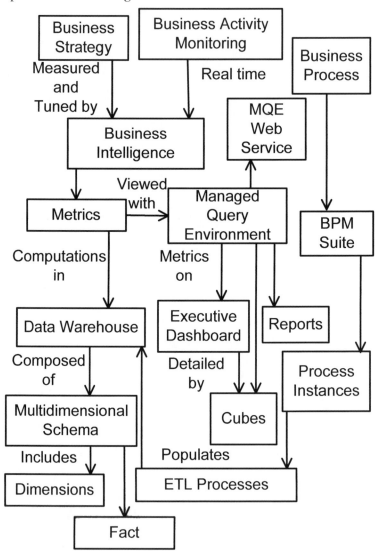

Figure 5.4 This is the concept diagram for Business Intelligence (BI).

BI is an umbrella term for a set of concepts and methods that improve business decision-making by using a fact-based system. BI supports business strategy by creating a tool for measuring and tuning the outcome.

A *metric* is a formula of one or more facts that is useful for managers in deciding on or checking the health of an area of responsibility. For a data warehouse to be a BI system, it must provide consequential metrics. An example in our case study might be the percentage of target leasing days for a specific month and a given equipment type.

The *data warehouse* is a set of database tables that hold the dimensions and facts—the MQE—and the processes that populate and manage the data.

A *multidimensional data schema* is a set of data that has been designed to compute summaries of facts according to many dimensions for a needed timeframe. For instance, Sumter sales revenue might be totaled for the company by region, equipment type, or others. The data is designed for dashboard users to look for trends and outstanding information.

A *dimension* is a holder of descriptive detail—including types, categories, or named entities—from the business ideas. Examples of a dimension from the Sumter business case are: equipment types, maintenance types, and sales division. Examples of *named entities* would be a customer, a store, or a reservation.

A *fact* is a numeric attribute that is associated with a dimension. Facts are also called measures. Examples are quantity, size, and duration of time.

An *MQE* is a suite of software that provides user-friendly, easy access to the dimensions, facts, and metrics. Examples are Cognos and BusinessObjects. BI happens when you use these tools to support the executive decisions. The executive dashboard is a graphical presentation of metrics that support decisions.

A *cube* refers to the mapping between the data that stores the facts and dimensions, and the information that describes the prompts and column headings (metadata.) The cube is a user-friendly connection between a manager's point-and-click and the technical query. The cube might supply facts that support the dashboard.

Software vendors use the cube term for a collection of user-selectable objects that give a query access to a source of data. Users look at the cube when they need to see a slice of data behind a dashboard control. The cube is a collection of data definitions, relationships, and other symbols that are stored in the BI repository. MQE software controls user access to the cube with security features.

MQE vendors provide Web services that work with other products in your architecture to produce important decision reports. The push of key findings to managers is often the result of BI. Many MQE vendors provide Web services that work with other products in your architecture. With BI Web services, you extend and customize business processes and business rules. MQE Web services also extend and customize reporting products.

DECISION FACTORS FOR SUMTER

To plan for the ideal inventory, we need to develop basic inventory metrics for rental processes. The executives decide on the size of the rental inventory based on a projection of the annual demand. Management matches inventory with demand for several quarters. In discussions with management, the following causes were noted:

- Excessive inventory leads to fewer days of rentals per unit
- Inadequate inventory lessens sales and increases overhead allocated to the equipment
- Demand varies from season to season

Simple accounting decides the basic rental charge for equipment. Sumter accountants base the rental charge on the total cost of ownership plus an allocation of overhead and the age of ownership. So, given these numbers,

- A unit costs $100K, including overhead
- History tells us customers will lease the equipment 60 percent of the time
- The margin is 10 percent
- Equipment life is 48 months

The daily charge for the equipment should be $126/day. Let's call the percentage of days in lease the Target Leasing Rate (TLR). Preferred customers increase the profit because they lease equipment for longer periods of time. This is the rationale for their negotiated discounts.

Once accounting has set up a rental fee for equipment, managers should oversee the total leasing rates. Leasing rates will predictably vary from season to season, so the BI system will need to compensate for this.

There are many different equipment types and equipment costs. The prices for a single equipment type increase yearly. Because it would not be popular to be constantly changing the rental fee, Sumter should rarely change the TLR.

Customers might rarely lease large expensive equipment, while ordinary bulldozers and motorized lifts may have high TLR.

As I mentioned earlier, construction equipment keeps significant value. Therefore, each equipment type has a target age—the best time to salvage the equipment, based on a combination of the tax benefits and the retail value. Even if customer demand remains constant, a certain number of units will need to be replaced.

Here are the decision metrics that BI will model:

- The target leasing rate—an aggregate percentage of the number of days equipment is leased to a customer
- Actual leasing rate—the annualized percentage of the leasing rate, computed for Sumter sales data equates to an aggregate of customer demand

You might also view these rates as the efficiency of the leasing process. A value of 1.0 would mean customer have leased every equipment unit.

PERFORMANCE METRICS FOR SUMTER

Organizations are successful with BI when they develop the goals and objectives that match executive decisions. The objective of Sumter's BI systems is to contribute to profitability by steering the company towards correct inventory. Because the economics that create rental demand change from quarter to quarter, an ideal inventory is impossible to achieve. Yet, Sumter wants to know where to set the inventory and how fast to get there.

Managers oversee business activities by comparing measurements of current activities against target (or baseline) measurements. The TLR is Sumter's baseline metric for monitoring rental inventory. The equation for the TLR for a population of equipment is:

TLR = SAF*(((TCO+ Overhead) / Daily rental Fee)/ Target Age)

where,

- (Seasonal Adjusted Factor) SAF = an integral of the seasonal adjustment factors for leasing rate
- Total Cost of Ownership (TCO) = The total cost of ownership including purchase, maintenance, licenses, and other fees
- Overhead = The local overhead allocated to the equipment unit, usually a percentage of the TCO
- Daily rental fee, the assigned fee for the equipment type
- Target age is the planned salvage age of the equipment, in days

During analysis, MQE software sums this formula for the equipment and chosen time range. The formula adjusts the TLR throughout the year. So, the software estimates daily changes in demand with a regression of sales data. For instance, different holidays that have low leasing activities will adjust the target lease rate. When the BI software computes the metric, it also computes the SAF in the analysis period.

The cost of rental for the equipment varies by customer and retail store. Preferred customers boost the leasing rate by leasing more equipment for longer periods of time. To improve leasing rates, store managers offer discounts during seasonally slow periods. Managers evaluate the rental activity performance by comparing the TLR against rental sales. A formula computes the Actual Lease Rate (ALR):

ALR = (Total Leasing Days)/Number of Units

where,

- Total Leasing Days = The days the unit was assigned to a paying customer
- Number of units = Total number in the analysis

The BI team will design the data warehouse to be able to support these computations for any useful combinations of equipment types, customers, sales areas, and time boundaries.

INFORMATION NEEDED FOR SUMTER'S INVENTORY MANAGEMENT SYSTEM

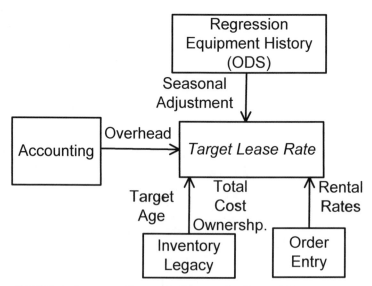

Figure 5.5 This is the concept diagram for Business Intelligence (BI).

Sumter's BI supports inventory decisions through an evaluation of the two metrics: TLR and ALR. Executives will use these metrics to evaluate the rental inventory levels.

The metric formulas need information from different systems in Sumter Rents. Figure 5.5 displays the needed information.

The BI team studied the sources of the information and decided that

- Rental days assigned to customers are available from the equipment history data described in Chapter 3. A regression of the data develops the seasonal adjustment factors
- The formulas also need rental rates for the equipment. The Sumter order entry system maintains the prices for equipment rental. There are two rental rates—the retail rate and the rate assigned to the customer. The TLR needs the retail rental rate
- The overhead for the total cost of ownership (TCO) comes from an account in the general ledger. Because cost and salaries vary, the overhead varies
- The formulas need the TCO and the salvage age of the equipment. These data are available from a legacy system

Similarly, the assigned leasing rate is computed from information in the operational data store.

The executive dashboard needs more than facts or numbers. It uses dimensions to focus on different parts of the business. Besides the entire business, the managers will want to look at metrics for a sales region, an equipment type, or a store. Also, the managers will want to look at the metrics across different time boundaries—last quarter compared with the current, last year compared this, and so on.

The dimensions gathered from different systems should be converted to one standard. The dimensions that span several application systems need data standardization. The BI team creates a uniform dimension set that is semantically correct and supports the business model.

In this information-gathering task, the BI team identifies the different systems contributing to the business model. The ETL processes get data for the business model. For each of the systems, one or more ETL processes might be needed. This analysis verifies the dimensions and facts that will be provided by the ETL process.

CONSIDERING BUSINESS RULES

Earlier, I described business rules as composed of categories, computations, comparisons, and controls. BI should incorporate this information into the data explored in the executive dashboard's cube.

Business rules are often designed to influence customer and trading partner behavior. Managers use BI to verify the effect. For example, special customer discounts should increase the equipment lease duration. Sumter offers corporate customer discounts to large companies with long leases.

BI discovers these customers. BI also continues to measure leases after the discount is negotiated. Some business rules are designed to influence customer and trading partner behavior, and managers can use BI to verify the effect.

A theme of BI, as carried out by the executive dashboard, is to monitor the big picture metrics. When performance is poor, look for parts of the business that underperform, and search for incidents, trends, and patterns that cause the poor performance.

To incorporate business rules into your BI, you should

- Identify rules that affect the metrics you are modeling
- Analyze the rule for redline values and incorporate these as dimensions in the data warehouse (customers with good credit, accepted quality measures, and so on)
- Extract numerical computations and add these as facts in the data warehouse

If you build your BI system with these considerations, your managers will be able to evaluate the effects of changing redline values and computations. This is another reason for using business rules approach. Because rules are centralized, it is simple to find the rules and use them to evaluate the decisions.

CONSIDERING BUSINESS PROCESSES

The equipment process logs location changes in the database. There are details about customer leasing, scheduled maintenance, and the time on the retail store lot. Between these, there are steps that take place. Store personnel prepare equipment for customer use, inspect equipment returned from the customer, and maintain the equipment.

We have three simple motions in the equipment. The basic system work flow consists of the following activities:

- The customer places a reservation for equipment. The equipment manager should prepare the equipment for the customers before they arrive to pick up the equipment. The reservation process records the scheduled pick-up time, and the equipment process records the time of customer assignment

- The customer returns the equipment. The ordering process records the drop-off time. The equipment process records when an employee enters the equipment inspection form

- The equipment process tells the managers when they should maintain the equipment. The equipment manager performs the maintenance and records this data

Business process suites write records of the dates and times of these activities. These are just three of the essential time records that should be watched. The BI team might add these time slices to the data elements in the data warehouse.

When your team builds a data warehouse in a business process environment, they should consider adding process scheduling data to identify other business events. The requirements of the business model will dictate the event definition. For instance, if we analyze shipping and receiving in an order entry process, some events may have occurred, such as the time between the order and a series of receipts.

To incorporate business process timing and performance into the data warehouse, you should

- Identify process activities that are connected to the business activity you are monitoring

- Find the source of timing records for the steps

- Incorporate the date or time variances into the data warehouse

BUSINESS INTELLIGENCE DASHBOARD

With the right combination of displays and controls, the BI team creates an executive dashboard that rapidly oversees developments at Sumter Rents. They should create a vision of the characteristics of a business monitoring environment—what managers see and how they interact with the analysis space. If the system is difficult to use, misleading, or filled with uncomfortable semantics, then it will not be well-received.

When designing an executive dashboard, the team chooses between dimension-based and measure-based controls. Because Sumter has many retail stores in many states, the team might use a map to allow the manager to select inventory metrics form several categories. The dashboard allows dimension-based controls when the manager wants to drill up and down. In drilling, managers use cubes to explore the multidimensional business model. Therefore, managers might want to see heavy crane lease rates in several states, then might want to see heavy crane rental in the entire enterprise.

A dimension-based dashboard has one or more dimensions and one or more measures. There are almost always at least two metrics in a control—a target or baseline value, and often also a historical value. When the historical value is above or below the baseline value, managers need to discover the performance issues. This is where they drill into details and slice and dice the information.

The managers choose dimensions in the executive dashboard, then select the metrics to compute from the executive dashboard. When they drill to the cubes, they explore the records. For instance, suppose rentals in Virginia are below the seasonally adjusted factor for the current month. The manager slices and sorts the details, perhaps sorting on poorly performing stores. If there are no poorly performing stores, the manager sorts by equipment type. The manager continues this activity until they understand why the conditions exist. In another scenario, a BI system might use measure-based widgets to show the status of one measure alone, or to compare several measures. For example, you might create a measure-based stoplight dashboard to show the status of one measure, or a measure-based gauge dashboard to compare several measures.

Measure-based dashboards do not always need a dimension. In such cases, the measures are totals for all dimensions in cube data sources. Because drilling is applicable only to dimensions, you cannot drill up and down on measure-based dashboards that do not plot a dimension.

Slice and Dice

The power of the cube is that the manager does not explore data with programming languages—the cube creates this for the user. The cube provides familiar business terms for the manager, not complex technical terms. The purpose is for users to think in sound business ideas and to be as easy to use as a dictionary.

As we mentioned, *slice and dice* and *drill actions* occur after the manager decides to explore a condition. Managers drill—or bring back data—from the widgets on the executive dashboard. For instance, a Sumter manager might discover poor rental sales in a state. The manager then drills to the detail. After this, they interact with the cube. In the slice and dice method of analysis, the manager uses tools to see data from different viewpoints and on different detail levels.

The aim of slice and dice is to analyze data by looking at different details and from contrasting viewpoints. Managers hope to gain ideas about the performance metrics and resolve problems. Query tools in the cube explore the detailed information associated with businesses events.

Cube data browsers have two modes—drill mode, and slice and dice mode. In slice and dice, managers alternate the positions of data in a report. An important slice and dice capacity is to be able to pivot data tables or move data from columns to rows. Slice and dice mode also

- Creates master detail reports
- Displays and selects data
- Renames, resets, and deletes blocks
- Changes tables and matrix tables into charts

In the slice and dice mode, users edit table data, including break reports, filters, sorts, rankings, and statistics. With a well-designed slice and dice layout, managers easily configure reports. They should be able to build a master detail report and reorganize this report by reevaluating the master, or by revising a master detail report.

The drill mode lets managers get new data sets. The information in the slice and dice data creates the drill mode. For instance, after the manager selects a master detail report, the managers might revert to drill mode and reestablish other data items as master. Through a series of actions with the cube, the manager might need to explore another side of the data set—thus he or she might redefine the heading of the master report. For instance, suppose a manager discovers a poorly performing equipment type at a store in the current month. The Sumter manager might drill across to other stores.

Cubes allow users to select various headings. For example, if the master header is the dimension *store*, the user can replace it with *equipment type*. In this way, the user builds many master detail reports. This query sequence enables the manager to see data on several detail levels.

Executive Dashboard Reports

Suppose Sumter managers notice that retail stores neglect equipment on the lot, resulting in decreased leasing days reported on an item. With the cubes the BI team has created, MQE software sends reports to the store's equipment manager to address the problem.

There is an even more interesting development in the industry. With MQE Web services, the BI team could incorporate complex conditions, evolving many metrics into business processes and business rules.

Security

Security systems in the MQE software control access to the executive dashboard. Usually, local utilities briefly log the user onto the repository and evaluate which cubes are available to the user. If a cube file is not present on the Web server, it is imported. The user gets only the data they have access to.

MULTIDIMENSIONAL ANALYSIS

The dashboard needs data to compute the metrics, and managers need to see the details to explore the reasons for variances. The metrics will be computed with a query of the data for the part of the business the managers explore. The BI team provides the data by creating database tables to hold the information. Lastly, they create ETL processes to populate the data.

In multidimensional analysis, the team designs tables for events measured by the metrics. These tables become repositories of events and facts in the data warehouse. These centralized structures also might have details in associated, contemporaneous structures. Many dimensions are in the table structures.

For the inventory monitor, the key event is equipment location changes. The table is called the equipment fact table. It holds the state of equipment in either the retail store, in maintenance, or assigned to customers. There are several ways to design tables for the data warehouse. When the BI team designs this fact table, they group dimensions and facts into one data element. Information for equations is included in the same record of the fact table.

The easiest data warehouse table to build in the Sumter case would be a day-by-day log of

- What store the equipment is assigned to

- What state it is in—customer assigned, maintenance, or retail store lot
- If it is assigned to a customer, then all the leasing data should be in the record—the lease, the customer, and the rental rate

If information for the equipment event is not contiguous in the needed form, then the ETL process will need to convert it to the data warehouse table.

Time dimensions should be associated with each of the records of the operational systems providing facts to the data warehouse. Facts and time dimensions include customer leasing, retail store (idle), and the maintenance performed.

Figure 5.6 shows the equipment fact table. The solid arrows show dimensions that are in the table. The dotted lines show facts copied from other systems into the table. Every equipment item has an entry for every day in the table. This allows the managers to explore metrics down to the individual equipment item. The top of the figure portrays the time dimension. The granularity of the equipment fact table must have enough detail to support the executive dashboard.

In interviews with managers, it is learned that there are two horizons to this objective. In the near view, managers study the leasing rates for the current month. In the longer-term view, managers evaluate the annual performance of Sumter.

An evaluation of the other records showed these findings:

- Equipment location is recorded daily
- Statements of total cost of ownership, salvage age, and overhead assets are available monthly

When there is data for every piece of equipment, then not only do managers plan inventory for demand, they also find inefficiencies. Earlier, I mentioned that a bulldozer might sit idle for months. With this data structure, managers will be able to discover this.

At this point, the BI team creates a rapid prototype of the fact structure.

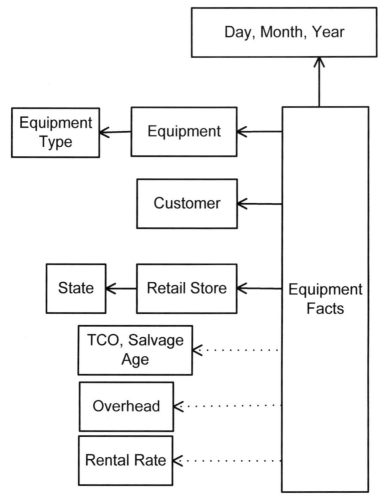

Figure 5.6 This is a simplified diagram of the equipment fact table. The diagram shows the contemporaneous nature of the records.

ETL PROCESSES

We have defined the dimension and measures for the model. We need to populate the data structures. Extraction, Translation, and Load (ETL) is the data processing activity of extracting data from diverse data sources, transforming the data, and then loading the data in a uniform format into a target data source. Your technical team might design and create the ETL programs, or you might use software to perform this work.

ETL is good to do with business process techniques, because most ETL software automatically decides when to insert or update records. The software is also written to work with large record sets.

Earlier, the BI team identified sources of information for the equipment fact model. Our equipment fact table has dimensions and facts from four separate systems. Because management has decided to use the executive dashboard to do business activity monitoring, the data warehouse should have current data. The teams design a composite, real-time process to get these data. In a composite process, one process gathers data across the systems.

The translation role of an ETL process might encode dimensions to one standard. For instance, we might have different equipment type codes in the legacy system than what is used in the operational data. The standard is the equipment types used in the operational data store. The ETL process standardizes the dimension. ETL processes for getting the data may be

- Batch extracts of the operational data, loading a flat file
- Queries of the data through JDBC or middleware
- Messages from another business process

ETL processes sometimes need external sources of data. Subscribing to economic information could be a Web service that is part of the process model.

BI PRODUCTION

At first, the BI team might quickly prototype the BI system with few automated processes. Programmers manually create, monitor, and refresh the data warehouse. They manually correct process errors. As the project goes ahead, the programmers become a part of the solution set because they understand the ETL process. Their manual procedures become part of the computing infrastructure. For the analysts and management, this circumstance becomes undesirable because valuable resources become tied up in repetitious chores. When the ETL process is in production, this circumstance is ended.

The final step of the BI project is production. The BI team has set up an executive dashboard that supports the project objectives. In production, the database needs to

- Scale to a huge size
- Report errors to the administrators
- Perform large operations in parallel so maintenance and refreshing of data might be efficient and timely

When the ETL processes load the data, the data warehouse has these characteristics:

- Process granularity—the ETL processes use isolated components that are executed in parallel
- Process control—a process hierarchy is defined and controlled in the BPM suite
- Intertask communications—the processes communicate with each other
- Errors reported should be controlled and broadcast

In production, architectural components are *hardened* for use. Here, the infrastructure is integrated through large-scale testing. Specific activities and deliverables include

- A database server, tuned for optimum performance
- Queries and views built during design that are tested and tuned
- Data warehouse distribution mechanisms that are designed, configured, and tested
- System backup procedures that are put into effect and tested

Much of the data in the data warehouse might hold sensitive information. Data might need to be withheld from groups of users. During construction, the MQE administrators create security groups and assigns users to these groups. The groups are limited to information that removes sensitive data from their view.

Testing

During quality assurance—or testing—the BI team should use a formal problem log that is available for the project leaders to review. This includes the problem area, suggested solution, responsible parties, and a suspense date for the correction. The project manager should review the problem log to discover trends and identify risks to the program.

WEB SERVICES FOR MQE

I have described how business processes use Web services to carry out business rules. MQE vendors, such as Cognos, provide Web service interfaces to their systems. This gives the IT team a powerful way to add complex conditions into business rules and business processes. With a Web service interface, a process or rule responds to complex or subtle conditions in the business.

BI is part of agile architecture—one that easily allows changes. Figure 5.8 suggests some of the features provided by combining Web services in an agile architecture.

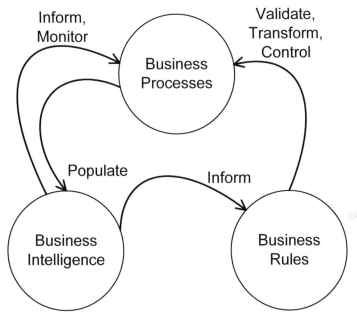

Figure 5.7 Web services and these technologies are essential to an agile architecture.

Figure 5.7 shows an extension of business processes, business rules, and BI. What is remarkable about these technologies is that there is an adaptable environment created with little traditional programming. When the Sumter technical team adds or changes a capability in one of these environments, they use modeling tools that model the business practice. The tools might be either a diagram of a business process, a business rule's goal, or a BI metric or cube. The tools also create or use Web services.

PUBLISH AND ACT ON THE RESULTS

Considering the dizzying array of circumstances builds a far-fetched case for optimizing Sumter's rental inventory. The accountants have computed a TLR for 700 types of equipment. There is a seasonal change to demand that complicates the speedometer widget on the BI panel. No wonder this was one of David Burk's (see Chapter 2) chief business challenges. The momentum of the success that Sumter has had in the industry might lull the managers into complacency.

Implications are clear. Aging companies might use the legacy of their success to continue operations while ignoring the complexities needed to fine-tune practices. Otherwise, they can use BI to root out the inefficiencies and plan. The choice is clear: Will you drive the numbers or will they drive you?

The key is creating a business structure drawn from the critical experiences of the operating past that provide the information for a better future. Second, the business environment is constantly changing in basic ways. The basics of economic theory are essential in every business, but the problems businesses face today are set in today's frameworks of beliefs, technologies, and radically lower information costs than ever before. The secret of success is creating efficient businesses that readily adapt to changing circumstances. BI creates these tools.

SUMMARY

Here are the summative points of this chapter:

- BI supports executive decisions. You use BI when the enterprise needs to oversee the total performance of the operation
- Executive dashboards monitor historical and target metrics with expressive widgets such as speedometers, temperature gauges, and stoplights
- The data that creates the metric values should be available in cubes. Managers analyze cubes using slice, dice, and drill
- The tables that hold the data are developed with multidimensional analysis. In our example, we built a fact table that held all the dimensions needed in one row
- Data are populated by ETL processes. These processes are well-suited for the BPM techniques described in Chapter 3
- BI software has Web services powers that extend business processes and business rules in novel ways

REFERENCES

Levinson, Meredith, 2004, "The Brain behind the Big Bad Burger and Other Tales of Business Intelligence", CIO.

Kimball, Ralph, 1996, The Data Warehouse Toolkit, Wiley

CHAPTER SIX: IT CONVERGENCE

BPM offers a powerful way to manage your legacy systems. If you have many legacy systems and many systems administrators, then there is a good chance that much of what they do can be managed by BPM software.

To convert your legacy processes into a BPM environment, you should consider adding controls, error reporting, and logging standards. This development effort is not extensive. The controls I suggest adding are the ones that your organization does manually.

There is an obvious place to consider using business process and business rules technology—look at the way your personnel manage systems and process data. After years of development, testing, and postproduction support, many enterprise information systems have become a myriad of processes, data loads, and extracts. These can become difficult to support. These processes feed COTS products, data warehouses, and other parts of your technology stack. Many organizations are dependent on a team of technical personnel to oversee and control this complicated environment. The weight of these challenges complicates adding new capacities or improving service conditions for your users. In this environment, there is a driving need for control of the processes that is accessible by nontechnical managers and administrators. BPM can meet this need.

BPM tools (Tibco, Intalio and WebMethods) can be used as a business-integrated scheduling and control solution for data processes. Most BPM tools can offer Web-based process controls that centralize all procedural business and data processing needs. This is called *IT convergence*. They do this with simple, consistent applications. Through gateways, BPM supports processes that are written in all types of languages—including Cobol, PL/SQL, and Java—in a way that nontechnical personnel can control them.

Managing a complicated legacy environment can be overwhelming.

I call the centralized process management tool the *BPM monitor*. Until all systems have become message-oriented and transaction-based, we must live with the legacy of decades of batch-oriented systems. The manager and business administrators understand the schedules and flow of the business better than the systems administrator or database administrator. Often, these schedules are fluid and changing, and in many environments only technical personnel can make these changes. The BPM monitors were created for this group to use daily. The manager is freed from going through technical layers to control the systems they own.

SIMPLIFYING ADMINISTRATION AND CONTROL

The inability to centrally monitor the internal state of processes can be frustrating for administrators. This is especially true when managing large data processes. BPM monitors can be configured with messages in the process control view. The BPM monitor depicts every process in the system with an informative snapshot. Besides automatically scheduling processes, BPM controls processes that are queued or running, and the manager can request an orderly stop to the process.

In IT convergence, business processes need not control every part of your system. It can be used on a pilot basis as a scheduling and logging tool for a subset of your processes. In fact, the BPM software can work *out of the box* as an interface to the queue management facilities. This approach, however, may not immediately help you improve the management of your environment.

Every complex application needs a master schedule that can manage all system processes. It should include all the controls needed to keep an application alive across many processes. The master schedule of processes should be available to all the administrators for planning and management purposes.

Most legacy systems were not natively built with a simple high-level view of their schedules and status. There is no one-stop shopping for the systems administrator to view the entirety of the processes that keep your application alive and well-fed. To do this requires surgery on the cryptic underbelly of the legacy system.

For instance, in an Oracle database, administrators must query and format the data that hold job information to view the schedule in a useful form. Further, the Oracle Queue (DBMS_JOB) table only describes the most current queue, it only holds part of the critical information, and it does not describe how the individual entries relate to each other. BPM improves control of these processes. After you have developed a schedule, you should be able to manually override the default process and reschedule for a warranting condition. With DBMS_JOB, you cannot see what a process is doing. To do this you must find the process identifier

(PID) and query the DBMS_SQL views and then relate the results with the process and what it is doing—a complicated task.

The BPM method communicates process information with simplicity through small additions to your legacy procedures. To manage the system schedule, you must be able to do four critical things—view the status, monitor what the process is doing, communicate with active processes, and view messages generated by the processes. Ad-hoc manipulation of a queue has to be done with cryptic (SQL*PLUS, CRON, AT) commands that your administrators might not be able to properly employ. All these actions are easily performed with the BPM monitor through a graphical, *point-and-click* interface.

BPM environments provide your managers and administrators with a master schedule that is independent of the features of the legacy systems. Business processes can be built for coordinated control. The processes will run uninterrupted until they are manually stopped. BPM and its simple development cycles create easily managed processes that can be gracefully shut down and removed from a queue.

Controlling key data processes with CRONTAB scripts on UNIX servers—or the **at** command functionality of Windows-based servers—can be inefficient and frustrating. The BCP simplifies this by establishing a method for consolidating and centralizing all processes into one application. The BCP allows administrators to schedule and coordinate individual process tasks on a proper timeline using its simple Web-based interface. Moreover, the results of each process execution are viewable from the Internet.

Nontechnical administrators have control over the schedule and frequency of execution of each process managed by BPM. They are not dependent on database and systems administrators to change business and data processes. It is also simple to change the business processes to manage dependencies and coordinate control, including process suspension when two or more processes interfere with each other.

A Process for BPM Control of Legacy Processes

Figure 6.1 displays a business process for moving legacy processes under the control of BPM software.

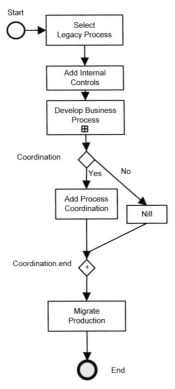

Figure 6.1 This business process shows the activities required to migrate a legacy process into the business process environment.

For each of the legacy processes, the team retrofits it with limited controls. They add a small about of code to the process. I call the legacy procedure with limited controls a *broker*. Next, the team develops a business process that runs the broker. The process for doing this is the same as that described in Chapter 3. If the legacy process needs to be coordinated with other business processes, then the team adds this coordination into the business process diagram. Finally, the team moves the business process into the production environment.

Concepts of Legacy Processes under BPM Control

Figure 6.2 show a decomposition of the concepts of managing legacy processes with BPM software.

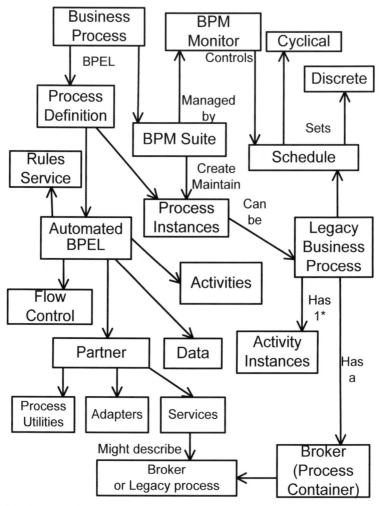

Figure 6.2 A concept decomposition of applying business process management techniques to the control of legacy processes.

A legacy business process controls a legacy system. If the IT Convergence Team adds internal controls, logs, and error conditions, then they are building a broker.

BPEL might define a broker as a service. BPM software can invoke many types of legacy processes through database middleware, COBOL gateways, and other APIs. If several processes need coordination, your team can build a business process that provides this coordination. Business processes can control a series of legacy processes or they can block other processes from running. The broker idea simplifies this.

Controlling legacy processes with BPM is simple. Managers can set and update the schedule of the process with the BPM monitor. IT schedules are either cyclical or discrete. A cyclical process is one that occurs in a regular time period. A discrete process is a process that runs on exact calendar dates.

PROCESS MANAGEMENT AND MISMANAGEMENT

Everyone uses processes that feed operational systems, ERP, and data warehouses. These might be scheduled or might be run manually. Global operations have forced the enterprise to be responsive over longer periods of time. The movement to Web-centric applications has increased this need. Data processing in this new world has become more than a matter of reporting—it is a critical business function that organizations cannot afford to mismanage.

The approach I am describing uses business processes in the BPM suite to control and integrate legacy processes in your environment. The system process—hereafter called simply a process—is a repeatable, procedural task that must be performed regularly or semiregularly. Every process has a beginning, an end, and an output, and possibly an error status. There are four basic traits you should consider when controlling a legacy process with BPM:

- Every process must be started and stopped—sometimes stopped before it has finished its work
- Every process should be monitored for performance
- Every process should produce an activity log
- Every process should produce a separate error log in case some exception or problem is met

In more advanced control scenarios, processes can start other processes or block them from running or being queued. This is an ideal application of BPM diagrams (see Chapter 3). BPM suites provide you with the tools to do this intricate management.

Your ideal system should function by breaking its objectives into focused, discrete processes that are managed and monitored by the system administrator. In a BPM environment, you let the owners of the processes service these processes themselves. You can group a series of related processes into a project and use the security provided by the BPM tools to grant access to the managers.

If your application's processes are not separate and atomic—that is, many missions and objectives done by a very few procedures—then you might wish to break these large programs down into many processes with more focused objectives. Suggestions for doing this are discussed in this chapter. There is no limit to the size of the objectives of single processes with a business process. You can use the API to communicate with the Web interface and see what the system is doing—breaking the process into focused parts will simplify the maintenance and operation.

USING BPM TOOLS TO CONTROL PROCESSES

If some or all your processes are scripts that are started by CRON or by hand, then these might be wrapped into Java to be scheduled with BPM. Most BPM tools permit system calls—however, you will have less internal control with that approach. Each of the processes might be enhanced with the BPM's API or a common database table.

If you are changing key system procedures in a production environment, then this should only be done after a testing and cut-over process. In building processes into a manageable unit, we define a broker as an extension of the process concept. A broker is a legacy process, invoked and controlled by a business process that is managed by the BPM suite. The legacy process should be adapted for control by the BPM monitor and administered from a central location.

To build a broker that is managed by BPM suites, the process team should do two things. First, they should wrap the legacy process in any language that is easily managed by the BPM suite. If the process is stored in SQL, then it can be called with a JDBC connection. Second, they should create a business process that controls and communicates.

Suppose you have a legacy procedure that loads reference data from one database into anther database. Previously, the program was scheduled for execution with an **at** command. The program is a stored procedure. To manage this with BPM software, all your process team needs to do is build a business process to execute the program. Figure 6.3 shows a simple business process for managing this.

Figure 6.3 This business process diagram depicts a light-weight, nondisruptive business process for integrating legacy systems. The legacy process is what I refer to as a broker. The clock denotes the schedule that is set by the BPM monitor.

This is the simplest method of using BPM software to manage a legacy process. Managers can change the schedule and view the history and status of the execution in this approach. I have found that most organizations require a bit more control than suggested in this diagram.

In more advanced scenarios, the broker can be scheduled, started, or stopped. It communicates with its environment through the software API. The business process supervises calls to the subscribing process. The broker's purpose is to lightly refactor the process. With a broker process, you only need to worry about the aim of the process, not how it is controlled by the administrator, or how it logs its success or failure. This control can be added with a few lines of code and should not intrude on the performance or the operation. Manipulating shared characteristics and behavior allows us to automate the management controls.

TYPICAL DATA PROCESSES

Most processes arise from the need to move data into the current system or out to another. Types of processes commonly encountered include:

Data Feed Loads. This includes the loading of reference data from legacy systems, FTP files from the Internet, and transactions in various formats into your application system. Individual or closely related data sets should each have their own broker. Data feed loads are commonly read with Cobol, C, Oracle's stored file utilities, or Java. Older processes might use older 3GL preprocessors. Most data loadings use a common source directory for incoming files, and a location for archived files. With flat files, data loads open the source, perform data manipulation, and then move the file into an archive directory. Some data files have record counts at the header. Proper loading of these might call for every record to be read properly.

BPM tools approach this pattern in a flexible way, because these tools can use the arrival of a file to start the process. You activate the services when the files arrive, then move it to where the legacy program can read it. BPM services can read the contents of a directory, open every file with a certain extension, and other useful directory manipulation schemes. Most BPM tools fully implement FTP.

Data Feed Extracts. This is similar to a data load except that the output is a file. Often the extract involves opening SQL cursors against many tables. As with data loads, the internal progress of the reporting or loading of a file can be difficult to trace without a monitoring tool.

ERP Transactions. Operational data are reported to open interfaces and gateways to post. These processes can be more complex, with the application of many rules, mappings, aggregations, and segmentations of data. The ERP process is often the most mission-critical application program. If your system loads ERP transactions, then managing this with a business process can be the first step in converting it into an LRT.

Report Generation. Time-based reports are commonly scheduled processes. These scheduled processes produce a report in a specific format using formatting tools.

Notifications/Messaging Email Notification. A key communications part of workflow is the transmission of email based on events and changes in the state of business activities. In the workflow, temporal business rules describe sequences of communications.

Data Warehouse Publishing. Many organizations create their own ETL processes to move data from an operational data store to the warehouse. These might involve many data manipulation language (DML) steps and cursors that aggregate the data for fact and dimension structures in the data warehouse.

As you consider these processes, you should see commonality with your system. If your processes are granular, then each one will do a named objective similar to the types shown here.

CURRENT PRACTICES

If your application is more than seven or eight years old, you probably see many layers of development artifacts in your environment. During the life of the application, developers have added the many types of processes listed above. As technology has developed, the practices for carrying out processes have also changed.

Earlier practices use a combination of DML in scripts and database-loading utilities. Shell scripts started the process with a simple scheduler such as CRON. These scripts exposed critical user names and passwords to the environment. Other variations of these early practices included running arcane tools such as SQL*FORMS in a batch mode.

More recent practices use Java stored procedures and PL/SQL procedures and middleware to do processing. This approach yields more flexible and maintainable applications. The caution is that today systems are not scheduled with consistent tools. Some environments use a mix of CRON, AT, and other utilities to manage their repetitious tasks. The challenge is to merge older applications into a modern environment.

MOTIVATIONS FOR PROCESS CONTROL

Enterprise systems work by breaking their tasks into many discrete processes that systems administrators oversee. Enterprise applications—those that feed operational systems, ERP, and data warehouses—use these processes to carry out much of their mission. A monolithic database refreshes data through triggers, replication, and stored procedures. There are, however, many design requirements that motivate asynchronous movements of data. Coordinating these processes can be complex without a standard approach to process management. BPM provides this standard.

Although a well-formed, normalized database is the mandated norm for operational systems, your organization probably needs data from diverse external sources. Thus, your designers create applications whose critical reference data are provided by other business systems. For instance, mobile transactions might need validation after their posting. Critical data elements may arrive from other data sources after transactions have been validated.

Enterprise Integration Systems (EIS) are often built to coordinate an application with the end-to-end business process that might not be present in other particular systems. One operation of the EIS is to add more business rules to the older system with the goal of lessening the manual steps that were involved in maintaining the system. For instance, two systems might have coexisted through the manual entry of different, overlapping data elements. The EIS can end the manual entry by centralizing the reference data and transactions. The EIS carries out these interfaces through a series of processes that load reference data and validate and correct the harmonized transactions. The goal is to create system processes that coordinate asynchronous states of data and stop the manual fixes that previously maintained the two systems.

Because today's applications run in a diverse environment, processes must be coordinated across many systems, environments, and languages. They use many types of data sources and outputs from XML, SQL*NET, or flat files.

For all of these reasons, most organizations are motivated to manage their business processes. We have already covered the steps for developing a business process in Chapter 4. What I am suggesting is that business processes can manage the system processes that you have in your environment. This lightweight approach to BPM can move the organization more quickly into this technology, without rewriting the most detailed processes.

LEGACY PROCESS CONTROL

Older processes were often written with a naïve sense of their shelf life. For years, developers used common UNIX methods on a server-by-server approach.

Besides the process tactics shown in Figure 6.3, you should consider adding mechanisms for sending commands to your processes through messaging or programming strategies. With messaging, you can build a flexible toolset for the control of the behavior and the activity of a broker. BPM monitors provide you with job queues that manage and run a list of processes on a specific timeline. With messaging, you can control this job queue by assigning a state to the broker. Useful states include

- GO—Allow the queue of this process
- KILL—Do not run this process, and stop it if it is already running
- ERROR—Do not run this process, an error occurred in the last run

Other processes can send kill messages, or your team can design a simple Web screen for this.

Figure 6.4 shows a more flexible approach to managing legacy systems with BPM software. To take this approach, your staff will need to add some code to the legacy programs. You can either develop a messaging strategy using the BPM's messaging API, or you can create a simple data structure for communicating with the programs.

Looking at Figure 6.4, the process starts to perform its duties when it is first queued onto a job stack by the BPM monitor's timeline specification. The schedule queue is shown as a clock on the diagram. Once queued, the process starts to perform its tasks by calling the broker. During its execution, the broker can periodically poll a message queue for its control signals. You should add code to each broker to respond to the *STOP* signal. The business process responds to the *GO*, and *ERROR* messages. The GO signal tells the BPM software to continue its normal management. The STOP signal tells the broker to stop what it is doing as soon as it can and return to control of the business process. The broker returns the ERROR signal to the business process. If the legacy procedure encounters a severe error, it will signal an error condition to the BPM software. This occurs when the developer of the application has included an error message from the process.

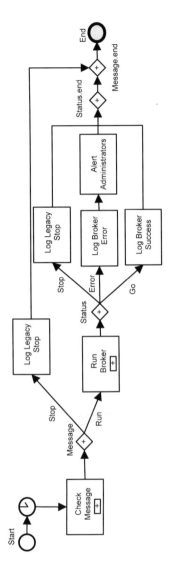

Figure 6.4 This business process diagram depicts a more robust way of integrating legacy systems processes.

For a process to respond to the *KILL* or ERROR signals, calls to the messaging API must be added to the broker. Besides responding to messages, each broker can be set up to send messages and write logs to the text files (the *outside world*) so administrators can quickly see what an active broker is doing or has done. The BPM monitor displays this messaging information and links it to the business process information.

When an active (queued) broker has finished its tasks, it will automatically re-queue itself to run the next time if it is set with a cyclical timeline, otherwise it will run on the schedule or on demand. This strategy gives flexibility to administrators to create a schedule that meets complex needs.

For a broker to be *active* (and therefore fully automated), it must satisfy two conditions. First, the BPM monitor must queue it. Second, it must have its state set to GO. Under these conditions, the broker is performing tasks regularly and is considered *active*. For a broker to be *inactive* (and therefore not scheduled to run), the manager should dequeue it, or it will not be blocked by another process.

To deactivate an active broker, an outside command would need to send a STOP message. When the control signal is set to STOP, and the broker reaches its next polling point, it will see the STOP signal, stop its tasks, and return control to the business process. After all this has happened, the broker will be in an inactive state.

There are two steps to activating an inactive broker. First, the state must be set back to GO by a message or command. If the administrator wishes to run the broker immediately, they must start the process at the BPM monitor. When enabling an inactive broker, the administrator must ensure the control signal is set to GO before queuing the broker.

Broker Event Logging

The broker should log the results of an individual run of the process including errors, notes about the start and end of the process, and detailed debugging messages. To identify vexing issues that are difficult to reproduce in a development environment, you might use controlled debugging of the application in a test or production environment. Debugging messages might be put in the log or displayed using a separate part of the API. Either way, broker logs are viewable from the BPM monitoring and the BPM software can set the debugging level.

Email

BPM software provides detailed, active control to the administrator. Some administrators, however, might wish to have direct warnings of issues and failures. Your team can add steps to the business processes to tell managers of selective process events. If a broker fails and is set to the ERROR status, you can add an email client to the business process client. Each member of the list assigned to the broker will get an email message. This allows pagers and cell phones to get messages. A business process can tell an administrator when its work is done or has failed for some reason. This cuts the on-site monitoring workload of the administrative staff.

MIGRATING LEGACY PROCESSES TO **BPM** CONTROL

When the technical team in your organization is building a new operational system, or meeting new requirements, they should use BPM techniques (see Chapter 4).

You can combine new and old processes in the same enterprise view. The BPM approach develops processes that meet their immediate needs while coordinating their results with legacy processes. By using a disciplined control process, you will achieve uniform error handling, process logging, and event posting. This combination will raise the productivity of your systems administration.

The project team should catalog each legacy process that must be managed and decide where it fits in the larger business processes. Categories of old processes should include loading data from external systems, workflow objectives, ERP transaction loading, and data warehouse population. By moving these to BPM control, you will start to understand their relationships.

Error Planning

When working with external systems, you will need robust, detailed error reporting to oversee the operational systems. You should develop error standards for each of the processes you migrate to BPM control. This includes when and where errors are reported and a process for tracking and recovery. With external interfaces, inconsistencies in design assumptions (file formats, maximum record counts), critical failures, and errors occur from

- Problems with database and operating system resources
- Changes in external operational systems rules, file formats, and transaction standards

Moving your process control into the BPM environment centralizes standard error events. Systems administrators and managers receive immediate warnings.

Normal errors for a process might include changes in expected input, a lack of disk space for table spaces, archived logs (or anything needing disk space) or archive copies of files, and exclusive locks on tables needed for inserting. You can use messaging to raise error events. The message should state the error that occurred, when it occurred, and what program or operation and lines of code caused the exception. The report also might include data that caused the error.

Large Amorphous Packages

Lengthy programs that perform many objectives and wander across the requirements are commonplace—particularly those written over eight years ago. Factors that create this include

- The skill of the developers involved
- The use of anonymous blocks of code before stored packages
- Undisciplined corrections and additions

There are many advantages to breaking these into more discrete units:

- A process with one goal is simpler to understand and maintain. It is easier for a new developer to swallow smaller units of your application
- A process with one goal is easier to debug

Separating the process into more discrete steps needs a code walkthrough and manual reverse engineering of the functionality of the code.

If you work with large anonymous block of code, you should wrap the block into a development environment that you can control. You can use debugging procedures to watch the application advance in a test environment. Combining messages with queries of the process results should clear up any ambiguity in what the procedure is doing. Look for parts of the code that carry out process steps in the large block. You might find redundant code that threads a process dependency in the single package. At the conclusion of all these steps, it should not be time-consuming to separate the procedure into more discrete steps.

MANAGING LEGACY PROCESSES WITH BPM

The BPM can control all the processes in the enterprise. BPM software logs broker-queuing activities, monitors changes in process control, and manages the job queue placement of the process based on the process schedule.

Broker Timeline

BPM monitors can control the timeline of most scheduled processes. The scheduled process runs on a timeline that is ether a fixed time between completions (cycle), or on a specific date and time (schedule).

A cycle or process cycle is the time between each execution. For instance, you might wish to start a process that polls for a database transaction or message every five minutes. Once the event occurs, it might take longer than the five-minute cycle to process it. The business process does not start the program while the current process is running, so the execution time is not in the individual time cycle.

- Examples of cycles include
- Load transactions every ten seconds
- Archive the transaction table every two hours
- Back-up every 24 hours

In a schedule, the process starts at each date and time in a list. There might be several entries for the business process to run. Example schedules include

- Produce sales report Monday at 10:00AM, Monday at 06:00PM, Friday at 10:00AM, and Friday at 06:00PM
- Replicate a large database schema on Friday at 11:45 pm, and on Wednesday at 00:15 .

You will find that the choice of using a cycle or a schedule is simple. If you are *polling* or *looping* for an event, such as the arrival of a message or a change in the value in a table, then a broker should run as a cycle. Your managers can manually schedule a process that needs to run at a specific time.

Legacy Process Dependencies

After you have connected the legacy process with a business process and the suggested internal controls, it is simple to set up dependencies with other legacy processes. A process might start another run after successful completion, or yet another after meeting error conditions. Processes might also stop other processes from running, and either requeue them or leave them in a suspended state. To carry out these activities, you build and deploy business processes with these capabilities.

One form of a dependency is *process-blocking*. If there is a nearly continuous (or scheduled) process that must be stopped while another batch program is run, then you can build a business process that permits you to block the first program while the other program is running. Figure 6.5 shows a fragment of a process, (Process A) that blocks another process (Process B) from running.

After it has been blocked, the process might either restart it, or it can be left off and wait for a manual restart by the administrator. The first scenario is used to prevent transactions from flowing into the system after a cut-off period. After the work is finished, the blocked process will be restarted. In another scenario, a process that was run because of a failure might block another process from running, thereby avoiding the corruption of data and activities.

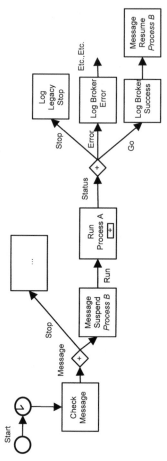

Figure 6.5 This business process fragment depicts one process being suspended by another process, performing its work, and then resuming the process.

SUMMARY

Using BPM to manage your legacy systems lets you continue to run systems and systems interfaces while introducing standard controls. Through IT convergence, you can focus on a dramatic cut in complexity and application count. As your team develops with BPM, your organization can transition gradually, driven by business objectives, organizational patterns, and projects. Migrating legacy processes to brokers and business processes improves control. The business processes yields five distinct improvements:

1. Process control—the periodic, cyclical, or on-demand control of processes

2. Process prioritization—the starting or blocking of processes. Depending on the outcome of events, you can put more than one legacy process in a business process diagram

3. Log management—includes execution logging, debugging, and error reporting,

4. System coordination and database administration—the control of the server's current resources assigned to the process queue

5. Performance management—the ability of the server to use current resources to perform data refresh and respond to process and user needs

The BPM approach supports application administration by controlling (scheduling and frequency), prioritizing (blocking and chaining), and logging daily events that occur in the application, and relaying selective results to the managers and administrators. Database and systems administrators work with resources and components of the architecture of the application to balance the user's needs with the performance requirements of the process queue. The aim is to keep the data current and coordinated in a previously confusing portfolio of applications.

The primary benefit of IT convergence is a greater understanding of your systems. The minds and unwritten practices of the personnel control this knowledge. By replacing legacy scripts and manual coordination with business processes, you can reorchestrate transactions and data flows to support the transition.

CHAPTER SEVEN: TECHNICAL ARCHITECTURE

There are two chief design tools in the BPM/BR—business rules and Business Process Management software. Each software package supports engines that run the rules and the processes. Because these engines use Web services, they create an SOA.

The SOA features late binding and Web services—elements much needed by mobile computing. Mobile systems work with subsets of data in local databases. Mobile systems can still work when there is a discontinuity in network service, or where continuous service is not practical. For example, they can be on aircraft, ships, or trucks. A BPM approach can orchestrate transactions sent from mobile devices.

Challenges arise from today's enterprise integration problems. Businesses and government agencies aim to face these challenges with a composite application approach. A composite application can integrate multiple COTS packages, operational systems, and external trading partners. With so many autonomous elements, however, there will invariably be overlapping terms and practices. The first benefit to the business is the enterprise unification of practices where the *best-of-breed* COTS systems are chosen to meet specific process needs. Business rules unify the terms. Therefore, the BPM/BR approach is an efficient way of building the composite application.

A composite approach with BPM/BR can move an organization from a legacy system to the new COTS. This is referred to as a *gating strategy*. With a gating strategy, large organizations can lower the cost and institutional shock of cutting out a legacy system. BPM/BR is particularly good at gating legacy ERP to the new ERP.

BPM runs composite applications with loose connections to business rules, databases, user interfaces, and integration programs. Because it removes the dependences on the system running a process, maintaining the process is simple. It also simplifies the code changes by isolating changes in format, process steps, or system interfaces. BPM is important in two additional areas—data warehousing and process administration. There are three themes in the BPM/BR approach to the SOA:

- A business rules repository, connected to a business object server that positions rules for change, and Web services publish the rules for processes to use

- A business process engine and a process control capability that simplifies the control of business processes
- An integrated business intelligence, ETL processes take data from composite applications and populates a data warehouse

The SOA places business practices where change will be simple. The architecture isolates the functions of the technical architecture that offer performance improvements and economic benefits. For instance, the organization may wish to add a new COTS product, change a core process, or develop new business intelligence. By repeating these themes throughout the user interface, the process, and the data warehouse, the architecture can achieve these objectives.

BUSINESS OBJECT

In the first chapter, I suggested that BPM/BR is an evolution of older methodologies. The BPM/BR architecture has been molded by the experiences of organizations that construct applications for the enterprise. These previous methodologies presumed a particular architecture. For instance, information engineering created *modules* based on functional CRUD decomposition. Each module was directly connected to the database with a proprietary language. The presentation layer is tightly bound or even a part of the business rules layer.

Figure 7.1 presents the older style of applications. The figure shows two forms of the same process—*Process X.*

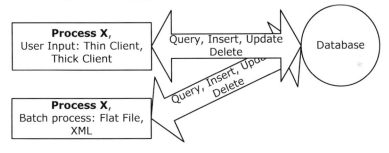

Figure 7.1 An example of earlier architectures with two different programs that implement the same process goal.

The top process runs with a screen and program code that query and update a database. This is the type of solution that might have been created by information engineering and CASE tools. The screen may be a thick client-server application with internal business rules and access to the database. Otherwise, the application may be a thin client Web tier with the equivalent code in the ASP, JSP, and HTML forms. The second box represents the same process, in a batch mode as implemented by loading a file such as an ASCII flat file or XML. The process could be a UNIX shell script, a C++ program, or something else. The point of the diagram is that this old style of writing programs was difficult to manage—it is hard to centralize your business rules when they are scattered among different processes. The programs may share development libraries, but this does not eliminate the diffusion of business rules because there are multiple calls to the procedures in the two processes. Even the use of Web technologies or XML does not solve the consistency issues—it merely recasts it in a different technology.

There are additional issues with the simplistic architecture shown in Figure 7.1.

- Scaling issues—multiple clients or sessions interacting directly (with no data caching) with the database can lead to contention
- Proprietary languages—the use of this architecture might put the business rules in a scripting language such as PowerBuilder, Delphi, and other tools. Even Web development tools such as Cold Fusion have their own languages.
- Inflexible architecture—any change to the database requires a change to the application. Any changes to the application require changes to the business process(es) in which it participates
- Poor security model—the security of the application is dependent on a system that may not be directly connected to the process. For instance, security may be an attribute of the database server

This was a fragile way to develop applications—changes in the requirements can inflict violence to the production code.

Isolating the Business Rules

Figure 7.2 shows a more robust approach to developing solutions. In this architecture, the two processes communicate with a common business object through a common set of messages. The business object performs all of the business rules validation and controls the access to the database. Actions performed by the business object are governed by the security certification of the calling client.

Figure 7.2 displays an early version of the loosely connected architecture. The business rules are positioned for change because they reside in the business object on the server. In object-oriented parlance, a business object is a business use case. Traditionally, business objects interact with data objects. Figure 7.2 shows the data objects residing in the database.

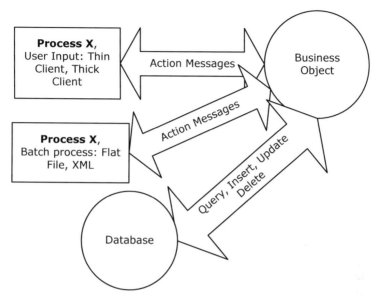

Figure 7.2 A architectural solution to a batch and user process as implemented using a shared business object and a message structure.

Because the business object could be generated (not executed) by the business rules repository (BRR), they originate from a centralized source. A policy that might affect many business objects can be propagated by a change in the BRR. Finally, this approach truly supports collaboration and reuse.

The business object approach shown in Figure 7.2 is better in the following ways:

- Better performance—the business object strategy can use threads and caches
- Improved, yet inflexible architecture—most business objects strategies use code, not engines, to run the business rules
- Improved security—because no user access to the database is needed and the business object can be placed in application servers

The approach is less fragile than the simplistic approach of the past. Changes to database schema need changes to data access objects. Business rules are isolated at a single point.

The decoupling of the application from direct interaction with the persistence layer has been around for many years. The architectural approach in Figure 7.2 is further modernized by a BPM approach. In the BPM/BR approach, the business rules in our use case use activities that are a part of a composite application.

Isolating the Process

BPM/BR strives for the architecture shown in Figure 7.3. The business object is decoupled from the batch (or user interface) in the process by the BPEL server. The database is entirely absent. This is important because technologists believe that the database will play a declining role in the future. Someday, BPM software will hold all business data in the flow of the process.

Figure 7.3 This is architecture using a shared business object and a BPEL server.

The benefits of the architecture in Figure 7.3 are:\

- Services can be loosely connected through Web services or messaging
- Agile Architecture—because processes and rules are run by an engine, not coded or generated, they can reflect rapid change
- Rapid changes for business

Figure 7.4 shows a business process design that implements these ideas. This shows how the file loading process and the user interface share the same infrastructure. This includes a connection of the application to the ERP.

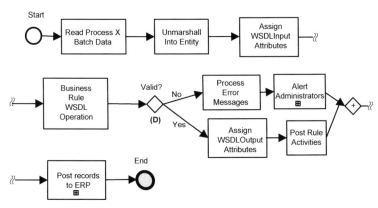

Figure 7.4 A business process modeling (BPM) diagram for a batch and user process as implemented by using a shared business object as part of a larger business process. The final step of the process is a posting of the transaction to the ERP.

Figures 7.1, 7.2, and 7.3 mark the evolution of application architectures over the last decade. The process activity shown in Figure 7.4 is part of a larger process.

INTEGRATING THE ENTERPRISE IT ECOSYSTEM

Today's enterprise architecture is a collage of operational systems, COTS, legacy systems, and data warehouses. With previous practices, such as screens placing records in a database (see Figure 7.1), IT organizations integrated these with fragile solutions. The IT ecosystem has been built up with relational data modeling, OOSE, client server, Web, data warehousing, and various types of ERP and COTS products. The result is an infrastructure with a milieu of disjointed programs.

To grasp the BPM/BR architectural concepts, it is important to comprehend why this new approach is needed. Architectures such as those shown in Figures 7.3 and 7.4 reduce this complexity. The aim is to change the way the application is integrated, updated, and managed. The application should be loosely connected to other parts of the enterprise system (see Figure 7.3) and everything should be a part of a larger business process.

Application integration is one of the top challenges facing business and IT organizations. The broad integration objectives of the enterprise should be supported by strategic modeling and process management activities. These objectives are the starting activities of the BPM/BR approach. Much of the evolutions of the early analysis are the outcome of different peoples' experience with developing, deploying, and then supporting eBusiness and application integration architectures.

Challenges of Integration

For many large enterprises, integration represents a large expense. The complexity and scope of information technology drive the high costs of integration. Organizations have been assembling standards and practices to simplify the challenges of integration, and software vendors are motivated to adopt these standards. Business rules and business processes are part of these standards and practices. They are the foundations of BPM/BR. Organizations include the Business Process Management Organization (*www.bpm.org*), and the business rules special interest organization, called the Object Management Organization (*www.omg.org*).

IT integration is a response to competitive pressures and the globalization of business. To participate, companies, organizations, and governments must become more integrated and connected with their partners and customers.

Prevailing economic conditions motivate businesses to improve efficiencies in all operations, including IT. These economics call for companies to cut product-cycle times and time-to-market, and to attend to their company's management needs. Mergers, takeovers, divestitures, and changes in regulations complicate integration measures. Today, companies have an increasing need to tie together their disparate systems in unprecedented ways.

To contain integration costs, enterprises must replace or reuse legacy systems and stove-piped operational systems. Programmers, however, never intended for legacy systems to be integrated. They never provided open interfaces or application program interfaces. To replace or combine systems, organizations have integrated or retrofitted their old systems with COTS technologies. These include Business-to-Business, Supply Chain Management (SCM) integration solutions and Customer Relationship Management (CRM) solutions.

In the software industry, there are many Enterprise Application Integration (EAI) technologies, including offerings from Tibco, WebMethods, Intalio and other companies. Some application servers such as BEA's WebLogic and IBM's WebSphere have EAI capabilities. Financial services, insurance, health care, telecommunications, and marketing have been early adapters of these.

The enterprise often runs on various systems. Over the decades, these have grown on different platforms using different technologies. IT groups built systems for specific business and technical reasons, and often for small divisions or departments. Legacy systems are frequently *stovepipes*—they are disconnected and fulfill meager purposes.

Other technologies in the IT portfolio can be COTS software. Sometimes new COTS packages and legacy systems have redundant capabilities. A massive investment in Year 2000 (Y2K) remediation gave many legacy systems new life. Legacy systems are on different platforms using different architectures, including Cobol IDMS, client-server, Web-based applications, batch, and real-time synchronous applications. Despite Oracle and DB2's marketplace dominance, applications use different databases. Depending on the age and type, designers created each data model differently. The result is a wide array of different transactional and process control systems. Each system has different data-entry styles, from the Web to batch mode.

From this, it is easy to see how the complexity of integration grows with the size and the age of the enterprise. In the United States Department of Defense (DoD), the Defense Finance and Accounting System (DFAS) is responsible for the accounting. DFAS estimates that they have over 400 legacy systems. This is the result of information technology that spans 40 years.

Besides architectural differences, integration affects many layers of changing technology. XML and Web services are replacing Corba and EDI. Vendor-specific middleware becomes antiquated with time. Styles of Web development have developed and bifurcated into many different approaches. Java Server Pages (JSP) replace Microsoft's Active Server Pages (ASP). The Java/JSP techniques can be even further refined with *open frameworks*. For instance, the Struts project abstracts the presentation layer from the business rules.

Because it is a self-describing and standard message format, XML has solved some of the semantic problems of EAI. But standard schemas in XML have changed slowly. In one industry, the enterprise may have to deal with multiple schemas. EAI needs to develop and provide transformation and translation between XML messages and between systems.

Even when they have built the enterprise from software from just one vendor, IT organizations still need EAI. In a single-vendor solution, one *universal* ERP manages all business processes. Despite available universal applications in a purportedly complete IT infrastructure, there is a set of secondary applications surrounding the ERP—quality, maintenance management, inventory control, and regulatory automation.

Most large corporations run with various ERP applications, including SAP, Oracle Financials, and JD Edwards. SCM includes i2 and Manugistics. Human Resources applications include PeopleSoft. CRM includes Siebel. Figure 7.5 shows some of secondary software that feeds the ERP. It includes fleet management, maintenance management, real estate, and various quality analytical or engineering tools. Some of these systems might be COTS. IT organizations might be responsible for some applications. Many of the stovepipe's capabilities are contained in the enterprise's COTS packages.

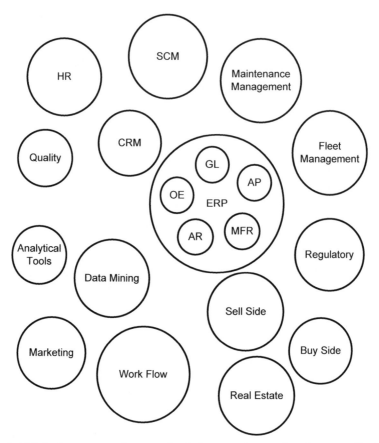

Figure 7.5 A high-level component diagram of today's enterprise ecosphere is a constellation of various applications.

For instance, Figure 7.5 illustrates an enterprise application ecosystem. Each application needs many combinations of overlapping entities. A small set includes

- Human Resources is the source for personnel—ERP, Supply Chain Management (SCM), customer relations management (CRM), Maintenance Management, and Real Estate all need these data
- ERP is the source for orders and customers—CRM, SCM, Sell Side, and marketing applications need these data
- ERP is the source of fixed assets—Maintenance Management, Real Estate, and Fleet Maintenance applications need these data

There are many more data needs. As the source system changes the data entity, the interface must report the change to the data consumers. To report these changes, the interface must transform attributes. In a point-to-point interface strategy, each application uses a different interface with different protocols. There is also a need to share information outside the enterprise. Each IT organization needs complex EAI across this hodgepodge of systems that organizations have installed over the years.

On the Buy side, companies have systems like Agile, Arriba, and CommerceOne. On the Sell side, they might have Seybold, Clarify, Onyx, or BroadVision. These systems have been built with different methods and with specific needs in mind. Organizations need to integrate these disparate systems.

Semantic integration unifies the transaction's meaning and context. Enterprises add special policies and procedures with a business rules approach. They can develop process flexibility with BPM. At the highest maturity level, process control creates autonomous processes, including mobile processes. Changing standards for BPM include the ability to publish and exchange business processes.

Clearly, integration is not an easy feat. BPM/BR techniques simplify integration problem domains in an IT ecosystem. BPM/BR uses a combination of the best practices that works with the technical architecture.

Historical Methods of Integration (Integration Through Retrofit)

In today's environment, there are two main approaches to integration. The older method is a custom point-to-point integration. I call this style of integration the *retrofit*. A retrofit occurs when programmers quickly insert the interface and heroically bolt it onto the architecture. The next approach is a business process approach that is integrated along a communicating backbone.

In a point-to-point integration, programmers retrofit each application with nonstandard custom business rules and processes. Next, they write programs for applications—data consumers that share data with the integration. This approach is costly and rigid to create and maintain. Without a centralized server, the integrations

- Apply the same business rules in different applications and languages
- Perform processes using different reporting or logging standards and methods
- Control the processes with different scheduling and coordination strategies

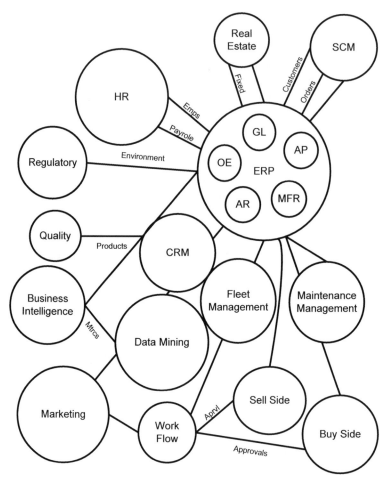

Figure 7.6 A point-to-point approach is developed with a narrow focus on the integration needs of the organization.

Every year, the enterprise also adds new technologies. New systems need to be connected to other systems. When the IT team adds BI to these new systems, they retrofit the data with ETL modules. When anything changes—data, business rules, or processes—the IT team changes every affected application.

Point-to-point integration projects narrowly address a goal. They create integration points that are fragile or unbending. Over the long run, they are more expensive to change. The point-to-point approach is redundant and inefficient. In summary, this is a costly, time-consuming, and invasive approach. Point-to-point integrations can be a large part of the enterprise's IT budget.

Taking the strategic approach—one that is more configurable—calls for an early investment. Yet, as processes and business rules change, the investment will pay off. Each business process might involve procedures and transactions across some systems. In the BPM/BR, managers direct the integration systems over time as part of a centralized decision-making process. The IT teams carry out the interfaces one-by-one and design them to fit into the long-term plan. In a 2002 study, the Gartner Group reported that organizations using a strong business rules approach experienced a large reduction in IT costs. The key to using BPM/BR is to plan strategically—companies should develop a long-range plan for loosening the connections between applications. Next, they tactically develop the first of a series of integrations using a BPM/BR approach.

The Role of the Operational System

All organizations, even those that extensively use commercial software, develop some custom applications. For instance, an enterprise might create a special Web-based application for an ERP's order entry module. I call this an *operational system*. Operational systems increasingly handle the integration needs of the enterprise. Software vendors and Open Source products provide sophisticated, comprehensive solutions to business problems. Operational systems tend to focus on the branded product line and customer services of the business.

In the Federal government, organizations are mandated by the Clinger-Cohen act to secure commercial products and integrate their practices with these products. The operational system's nature is changing. The Web screen connected directly to the database is less likely to be written—the enterprise is devoting its resources to core integration and business rules efforts.

The Composite Application—a More Strategic Approach to Integration

BPM/BR loosely couples programs to the architecture. Web services interact among presentation layers, integration processes, extraction and translation processes, and BI applications. The BPM or business rules define the protocol for every layer or application. The result is comprehensive interface specifications for processes and business rules. These specifications explain how to communicate with all the applications.

One long-term goal of this approach is to standardize every application's business rules so that IT teams can reuse them across other integrations. Everyone should know where rules are and how they are used. In the enterprise, a developer should be able to explore a server(s) Web services directory to find out how to use a business rule set.

Centralized business rules cut the cost and improve the flexibility of connecting all the applications. The enterprise can lower costs by selecting Open Source technologies or using a competitive practice in a COTS package. Through the business rules services, they then add their *cultural fingerprint* to rules by feeding transactions and integrations to the COTS packages.

All BPM/BR activities are managed in the business rules/process (BPR/BRR) repository. In the rules repository, there are reusable components, including

- The way data formats are defined
- The *signatures* of the business object (the way it is used)
- The data mapping and functional tools

The BRR simplifies building interfaces to other applications by creating common business objects. Delivering the business object from the BRR is just one advantage of the strategy. More improvement for integration with the BPM/BR includes

- Applications running in BPM software might use real-time and batch integration. Teams can convert a point-to-point solution—which only supports batch mode—into one with real-time characteristics
- The environment can change rapidly
- The BRR creates mappings that connect to enterprises outside the organization for B2B and SCM integration as well

BPM creates real-time visibility and asynchronous control of multistep business processes. Businesses that do this easily adapt to new applications and organizational changes.

Integration with Trading Partner's Systems

BPM/BR is not limited to internal systems. Its powers combine customer and trading partner applications and processes. For instance, the IT team uses BPM techniques to share processes with trading partners. BPEL is designed for this.

WDSL and BPEL are standards that simplify this exchange of process information with trading partners and customers. BPEL connects transaction validations against business rules through published WSDLs.

BPM develops a system without point-to-point integrations. The BPM/BR architecture creates applications at a lower development cost with higher manageability of integration requirements. BPM incorporates the specifics of the operating systems, security issues, the standards involved, and the technologies. It supplements the scope by refactoring legacy systems. Each project contributes to a centralized business rules server.

Figure 7.7 presents an abstract outline of a BPM/BR approach to EAI. The figure shows three layers of application integration—enabling one application to talk to another. The core components enable

- Connection to the applications—when it is through a WDSL, there is a *w* inside a circle
- Validation of the transaction against a business object that is always published as a WSDL
- Transformation of passing message attributes, or a change of the message into a form understandable by the application, as denoted by subscripts
- Control and management of the data flowing between applications

These are parts of the BPM/BR architecture. General design considerations include

- The way the services are invoked
- Supporting technologies
- The sequencing of the actions

Legacy systems often support batch processes. Your team might design a messaging scheme through a process that spoofs the transaction.

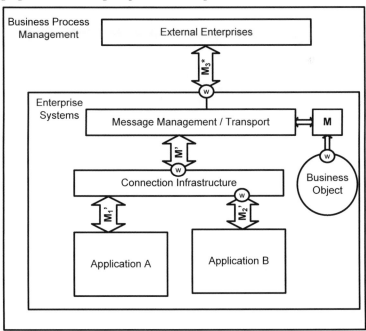

Figure 7.7 The powers of the BPM/BR platform support SOA: Web services and messaging.

One layer of Figure 7.7 is the B2B integration. This layer connects to external enterprises using their security and protocols and enveloping. The two applications act as a composite. The message M is a request for some operation in the two applications. The process translates the message and directs it to the correct internal application and external applications, as in a B2B scenario. The business object processes the rules. In this example, the message is bidirectional. The transport layers translate the message into a form that can be consumed by the applications. BPM controls the nature, timing, and the message flows.

In a composite application approach, BPM integrates many participants, including different systems and users. Managers use BPM software to oversee these processes as they run. To implement this, each application needs an adapter component loosely shown as the bidirectional arrows. The adapters are responsible for communicating the proper style and content.

Integration Messaging

A messaging approach for integration is needed to build a loosely connected infrastructure in a few situations, such as with

- Mobile processes that are not a part of the enterprise network
- Interfaces for complex, composite applications where Web services would be inefficient

The communications infrastructure or middleware is responsible for sending messages to system to integrate and control. As shown in Figure 7.8, there are four major communication patterns between systems in a message transportation system.

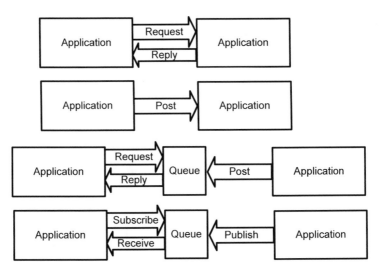

Figure 7.8 There are four styles of message-passing in EAI scenarios.

The first pattern is request/reply. This is similar to the use of a terminal/database application. From a systems perspective, a process sends a request and then suspends processing until it gets a response back. This is a synchronous, or time-sensitive, process where systems, such as within a data processing environment, must be online while it passes the message.

The next pattern is simple message passing. An external system sends a document, such as an EBXML request, for an order of products. Next, it gets a confirmation of the request. Unless an error occurs, there is no more business information returned. Just as in the first style, this is a direct system-to-system communication, and the synchronous, direct message-passing requires that the systems be online.

The next two patterns use messaging queues to support an asynchronous form of messaging. The queues serve as staging locations between systems. With simple messaging and queuing, a message can move from application to application with certainty, even when the target system is *not* online.

A more advanced technique is to employ publish-and-subscribe messaging. This assumes a loose coupling among the systems involved. This technique is implemented in Sun's JMS and in Microsoft's .Net. It is similar to an email client such as Outlook. For instance, an application publishes a message object to a queue, such as a shipment notice, and it need not know the details of the final recipients of the message object. Receivers register themselves as subscribers that pull the messages from the queue. The advantages to this are the few dependencies between the publisher and subscriber. Applications, for various reasons, can dynamically add or remove subscribers. Therefore, if the new system is updated with shipment notices, they subscribe to the messages.

Broadcast and subscribe is increasingly being used to loosely couple systems. The messages need to be translated and harmonized among the different needs. This core capability is provided by a business rules engine. It transforms and formats the message, while process management routes the data.

Business Rules in Message Translation

The business rules activity defines what a business does and processes define how it integrates this into the architecture. Applications and the processes that monitor and control them often have different data structures and application interfaces. Messages pass from application to application in several different ways. The business rules architecture transforms the messages and applies rules. The business activities process the business rules and transform the data from a central source. The first translation is syntactic. This is a reformatting, parameter by parameter, of the message into a form acceptable by the target system. Transformation can be as simple as a date change, or it might certify each of the supplied parameters is in the proper format.

Business processes intelligently route data among systems. When a sequence of business activities runs, the system interprets its contents and then orchestrates related systems. Business rule transformations meet the semantic needs of the process. Based on the meaning of the data, semantic rules alter the data, apply constants, and derive attributes. Rules perform other translations. For example, a rule might translate an attribute from a local standard to an industry standard.

The BRR maintains a common intermediary and independent format between the applications and systems. This is known as a canonical format. You use the canonical format to cut out point-to-point interfaces. Canonical rules translate the message from X to Y, which is the canonical intermediate format, and then on from X to Z. The point-to-point design converts a message from X to Z. Canonicals decouple the format of the messages passing between the systems. This is similar to the messaging queues that decouple the message transport. With canonicals, a change to System X should not cause a change to the other data consuming systems—it is isolated by this intermediate message format. The purpose of this modeling technique is to create layers of abstraction that isolate changes in systems.

Users of COTS software configure data to meet enterprises data needs. These are known as *flexfields* in Oracle financials. For instance, many organizations use SAP's physical plant module to perform fleet maintenance. The SAP application is configured with the fields needed to turn the generic equipment into a vehicle. With this flexibility, an organization configures the COTS to display their own fields and carry out customized business practices. What is missing from these fields is a way of validating and translating the fields with business rules. Business rules can manage these data. Through interfaces, an enterprise can add its own business rules to these configurable fields and reflect their needs in the application.

Data warehouses need to subscribe to the business information in the messages. By using a messaging backbone, a process can catch and perform ETL of the information in the systems.

A Unified Interface

Ideally, the BPM/BR SOA carries out processes in one interface exposed as a Web service on the Internet. As needs arise, such as creating a new product offering on the Web, IT teams easily design new systems with centralized business rules and processes.

We have discussed message transport and transformation. The next topic is the interfaces into the applications. There are several common interfaces

- Batch mechanisms, such as FTP file transfer
- Transactions or real-time requests through HTTP or direct TCPIP communication

Like the core process I discussed in Chapter 3, interfaces should be language and platform independent. This is the reason the SOA is so important. Combining WDSL and BPEL can enable

- Unified interfaces that handle the application connectivity
- Data transformation
- Intelligent routing for the transactions and messages passing between systems

With SOA, each intermediary and adapter communicates with other applications. Where needed, message queues perform the work. The work can include putting in orders, updating records, and so on.

Integration with the SOA hides the complexities of different operating environments—communications and protocols. This is the advantage of using a framework based on WSDL and BPMN. Integrating systems with ERP is similar to integration into a legacy COBOL system that looks similar to some other integration.

As companies try to compete and outmaneuver each other for market leadership, management of the supply chain is increasingly important. B2B integration has become essential. In a BPM/BR approach, these systems can act like sending and receiving mail. The communication with an external entity needs partner management. In one scenario, imagine a parent organization with many divisions. The system must send many transactions in many protocols. The system would need to manage the protocols. It sends and receives EDI, Rosetta Net, or Biztalk messages back and forth. The adapters have to manage message authentication to ensure it is directed to the correct destination. Message encryption and decryption protects the message contents moving across the public Internet. With transaction message nonrepudiation, all parties agree on what was sent and received.

For example, a customer sends an order. The B2B component de-envelopes it. Based on the protocol that was used, the process authenticates that it came from a partner. It decrypts the contents. Business rules validate it for formatting according to the protocol. More rules apply to the transactions in the message. Process management moves them to the correct application. Finally, the process returns an acknowledgment response to that customer. Everyone knows that everything was successfully processed.

One of biggest challenges of B2B is the high cost of adding trading partners. For instance, 80 percent of suppliers have been historically unable to use EDI because of this cost. The methods, different technologies, or lack of infrastructure in place has prevented them from supporting an expensive EDI system. For businesses entering the new world of XML and B2B, rapid adoption of these technologies establishes liquidity in marketplaces. BPM/BR yields rapid on-ramping of small-to-medium enterprises.

THE PROCESS INTEGRATED DEVELOPMENT ENVIRONMENT

The previous section talked about how organizations used to develop integration and the ideal they are striving for now. I am going to tell you how the BPM/BR can be used as a method for building the environment you need. In the previous sections, I inferred that

- Point-to-point integrations are a fragile way of developing applications
- Tight bindings to the database is one point-to-point integration technique
- A messaging, EAI architecture offers an environment that hosts loosely coupled activities in the business process environment

The BPM/BR addresses many of the challenges in building an EAI architecture. There are five components to the BRR Integrated Development Environment (IDE):

- The BRR that consists of the business rules workbench, the metadata repository, and the business rules engine

- A process server that runs the BPEL processes that the BPM team created. The process server might host the ETL processes for the data warehouse
- A data warehouse server that hosts the star schema as populated by the ETL processes in the process server
- A process management server that monitors, schedules, and coordinates legacy processes in the process server

These components align business and the IT infrastructure because

- They place business rules in one place so it is easy to change how an organization works
- New user applications, processes, and data warehouses can be quickly created updated or removed
- The processes can become a part of a business processes management strategy
- Interfaces to other systems as trading partners are simple to change

These architectural components are the outcome of the activities of the BPM/BR.

BPM

BPM is the outer layer of Figure 7.7. BPM manages information flows across the integrated systems. It works at a higher business level to simplify management control. Business managers and systems administrators control the processes. A business rule surgically adapts the data validation and transformations in information flows. Processes occur before rules. Therefore, an early activity of the BPM/BR is modeling the business process using BPMN activity diagrams. Business process modeling

- Unifies the business owners of the process and the technical implementers
- Enables the collaboration with systems needed for the composite application to work
- Identifies where and how business rules are to be introduced and enforced
- Standardizes how the exceptions and alternate processes are to be managed

Each activity in the process either requests the services of a partner or collects input from an end user. The end user can be an employee, a customer, or a partner. This may happen in a workflow scenario. As the process runs, each activity does the assigned task based on the business logic. When the process runs in a monitoring environment; the managers see an aggregated view of all data. This is independent of the differences in the systems.

A benefit of this approach will reduce needs for database services. As the process team configures LRTs in the business process software, they also configure the data (persistent storage). Business Process Query Language (BPQL) gets to these data elements. For example, a BPM creates one view of all the orders in a composite application. This is independent of the inventory systems or order management systems. The BPM team creates a single view of the business forms in the process diagram. Traditional data modeling is unnecessary. Therefore, the need for data modeling and database management will become a systems administration chore.

BPM manages exceptions in the business rules validation and the process. The BPM team can build processes that remove long-running transactions. This removal might involve a dozen different systems. This is referred to as the *compensation* part of the process model.

BPM manages all the data available in the process. This includes the data *between* the activities. An ETL process can provide this timing data to business intelligence analysis. For example, an analysis could identify inefficiency in a business rule for an interface to a legacy system. With a revision to the business rules or to the processes, the enterprise can add logic into the rules to filter those out, trap the inconsistencies, and increase performance.

MOBILE PROCESSES AND B2B PROCESSES

Global IP communication is becoming increasingly common. Different technologies are spreading wireless IP networks. For instance, Worldwide Interoperability for Microwave Access (WiMAX; IEEE 802.16e) is set to become the *next big thing* in the mobile technology world. WiMAX implements a Metropolitan Area Network. WiMAX allows users to connect to the Internet at broadband speeds while being many miles away from, and out of line-of-sight of, the transmitter. A less rich mobile technology is Wireless Application Protocol (WAP). WAP has become the standard for wireless *terminals* such as smart phones. Where do these technologies fit in with the three themes we have been discussing throughout this book?

As bandwidth spreads, the customer and trading partner act as virtually connected components in the composite application. Someday, the business process will support applications on mobile computers. Processes will spread economic information into the user's pocket—even when the application runs on a plane, automobile, or ship. This advancement will require many complex transactions to be processed.

Mobile applications present many challenges. For instance, mobile applications should not reveal sensitive or irrelevant information. If the mobile application is a:

- Trading partner, then they should only see their orders or contracts
- Customer, then they should only see their own data
- A local distribution point, then they should only see their own customers and inventory information

Data security is only part of the issue. We want to be able to develop an application that we can drop onto the mobile device as easily as we send a document.

The mobile enterprise will be able to interact with the composite application. Some of the benefits will be that

- In transit inventory becomes visible—where it is and in what quantities
- Complex sensors can be deployed and scanned for input
- Customer is continuously available—offering and orders are quickly routed to the customer and trading partner
- If business rules can be pushed, then changes in policies and procedures will be simpler to maintain.
- The task of knowledge management will be reduced

These are some of the benefits of application in a mobile environment. Even with a globally perfect communications network, connectivity is not widespread. This architecture will need a new technology—agent technology. In theory, agents can post transactions, and pass documents or information requests without the benefit of continuous communication.

Playing a role in the composite application, Autonomous Enterprise Agents (AEA) need business rules, reference data, and validation services. These agents communicate with other agents. The AEA might fail gracefully and arbitrate corrections for the user.

Because the connection is not always available, the agent or application must queue the transactions, prepare the queue for consumption, and arbitrate the failure of a transaction for correction. Systems correct the data at the enterprise or at the source. The AEA will need to

- Set up and arbitrate a service request
- Validate the transaction
- Move documents to the enterprise

AEA can refresh the local application. The AEA might use the services of the BPEL engine to interact with the enterprise. One activity might gather reference data for the AEA. It builds a queue and publishes data to the relevant subscribers. Services in this environment keep track of who gets that data, how long they need to see it, and when they get it. The business process coordinates with the rules engine to get the correct data into the reference data queue.

The native powers of the BPEL server can service the mobile process. Activities in the process can classify the types of replication that are needed to manage the rules required to implement an AEA.

SUMMARY

IT organizations should strive for a modern computing architecture. When there is a need for global operations, the team designs the architectural to allow a continuous, or 7x24, operation. Today's technical architecture is a combination of hardware, operating systems, and network software. Collectively, a BPM/BR strategy works as a series of loosely connected services. IT teams use the BPM/BR strategy to create applications that leverage these services.

There are many design choices to consider in building, upgrading, or modernizing the enterprise architecture. Powerful and complex technologies complicate the decisions. The team in the technical architecture activity selects the physical components for a loosely connected EAI environment. Your team should consider parallel or grid architectures for scalability and consolidation of outdated hardware, and single application servers. Another choice is the new, low-cost, high-performance systems. These systems offer improved operations and simplified backup and recovery.

Separate teams manage processes for many legacy systems. Until organizations modernize, the old ways of supporting these systems must be preserved. The BPM/BR strategy can improve the efficiency of the technical architecture. Modernizing the technical infrastructure with BPM can unify these teams and cut manual steps (see Chapter 6). BPM software can replace legacy processes with a centralized control and messaging tracking for traceability, encryption, and security.

Today's software includes many capabilities that lower development and production costs. Software for user applications and business intelligence includes database servers, managed query environments, Web servers, and portals. Increasingly high-quality Open Source solutions, such as Intalio or Openlexicon, are available for these.

A series of EAI, work flow, and document management applications support the core processes of the enterprise. There are many more capabilities in commercial application servers, such as BEA or WebSphere. Underneath this are databases, development frameworks, programming languages, and repositories. These tools are exquisite in their extensive and overlapping powers, but they require massive amounts of programming in Java or C++ to work.

BPM/BR software support B2B collaborations with very little programming. For instance, if a partner interacts with a contracting process in the enterprise, the transaction interacts with the business rules, which are run by a business rules engine and a business process, which are run by the process engine. The challenge in combining these capabilities is to select the solution set that best meets your design and support needs and is reasonably consistent.

You should consider the emerging role of wireless mobile devices. As global wireless networks improve, there are new opportunities for rapid data collection capabilities and software with tactical capacities. These remote devices need to use mobile autonomous processes and agents.

In conclusion, the strategic benefits of composite application include

- Application logic, functions, and features can be inserted, extracted, updated, and rearranged within a flexible, coordinated environment
- The functionality of existing applications within the enterprise infrastructure can be extended, regardless of whether they are packaged applications, such as SAP, Oracle, or PeopleSoft, or are existing legacy applications and systems
- Widely adopted industry standards can be leveraged to create a technology- and vendor-agnostic platform
- Business processes in a network of partners or internal systems can be connected
- Companies can adapt easily to changing customer needs and business climates rather than relying on manual integration or brittle point-to-point connections
- Businesses can configure and assemble Web Services to achieve tangible business value in months rather than years

Clearly, today's IT infrastructure is an environment in flux. Over time, management's goal should be to improve the productivity and cut the cost and complexity of operating information technology. More robust technologies must be added to the ecosystem to remove older or unsupported hardware and software, consolidate redundancy, create easier relations with trading partners, and take advantage of more profitable business practices. These technologies might include new COTS and operational systems acquired from mergers and takeovers. A simple vision is that IT managers should remove all the point-to-point integrations and replace them with technologies that do not require programming. The long-term vision is that all external components of the composite application will have synchronized, seamless access to the enterprise.

Data warehouses and the ETL that supports these should be automatically coordinated with changes to new business processes and rules. Managers should be able to implant special offerings or contract terms, and respond to competitive offerings in an unconstrained way. BPM/BR is a way of achieving this.

CHAPTER EIGHT: TRANSITION

Once the project teams complete the activities of business process modeling, business rules, BI, and IT convergence, they move the products into production. IT teams also need a fast and efficient changeover process when transitioning from a legacy business process or application. To cut risks, you should carefully plan the transition.

The following information is based on extensive experience with BPM/BR transitions. This chapter describes how to plan for a BPM/BR transition or migration. It will help your team in the change-over process, save you on unnecessary expenses, and highlight the stages needed for a smooth and safe process.

Four phases complete the transition process:

- Transition Plan—Your IT team should develop a thoughtful plan for moving the products of the BPM/BR into production
- Migration of Legacy Processes—Legacy processes might affect the transition process
- Testing and Validation—An independent validation and verification team tests new systems or updates
- BPM/BR Activation—After testing, the system migrates to the production environment

This plan assumes that you have installed the software components of the BPM/BR. They should be in the organization's development, test, and production environments. Setting up a BPM/BR environment is not a small chore. Administrators need to be familiar with the installation procedures and considerations of

- BPM Software—Intalio, and others
- BPM/BR Software—Fair Isaac, and others
- BI Software—BusinessObjects, Cognos, and others

They should learn the similarities and differences between the original environments. As part of the installation process, the managers create all new administrative jobs and tasks. The jobs need proper scheduling to maintain operation of the BPM/BR architecture.

TRANSITION ACTIVITIES

In the transition, the team prepares a system for the new or updated components. In mature systems, this should ideally be a simple matter of redeploying business processes and business rules. The systems that must be migrated should include development, testing and production.

Changes in business rules might require a migration of schema. If these changes mandate the addition or removal of data elements or constraints, then the database will need to change. Reports and stored procedures will need to adapt to changes in column names and constraints. For instance, process changes might phase out older batch processes. This calls for a cut-over to a more streamlined message—one with more succinct data elements. This can be a time-consuming and risky activity where larger databases are involved. The administration team needs to coordinate this activity with business operations.

During the migration, the old system will clear outstanding processes. This might take several days, or it might occur on a fiscal time boundary such as the end of the month.

As your application becomes more service-oriented, migration will become a simple task. Business rules tools can position predicate (If... then... else...) changes for real-time, in-line updates. For instance, if there is a threshold value that triggers a condition for a process, and the value is in a predicate, then you republish the rule in real time.

If there are changes to the application, database, or messaging structure, then you should write a migration plan. The migration plan should include the timing of database changes and a tactical plan for letting the production system cut over to the new environment.

Transition Planning

As a first step for success, you should plan the transition process. In earlier activities, the team documented old process information and potential logic conflicts. You also need to understand your organization's technical architecture.

The team transitions affected operational data stores or data warehouses. After that, the organization's IT team starts the conversion process.

A successful migration needs a competent team to administer, start, and use the new process. You should choose a team leader for the migration team. This team should include the current support staff, operators, production analysts, database administrators, product administrators, programming personnel, and security administrators.

In the BPM/BR or IT convergence activity, the process team documents the workflow of the old process steps. The BPM software manages the new process. Steps of the old process, however, need to be considered in the migration plan.

The migration team should develop a detailed maintenance schedule for the transition. The plan should identify the risks involved so it can assure system availability.

A process workflow depicts completion of the critical aspects of application management. This workflow identifies where the old process can be ended and the new one started. The migration plan should incorporate the Service Level Agreement (SLA) constraints.

Team Profile

The transition team should be familiar with the legacy systems features and operation. This includes the old system's methods of managing the environment, the site's rules, procedures, naming conventions, and clerical chores.

Previous Process Management Assessment

For a safe transition to the new applications, your team should

- Identify how scheduling processes are performed in the current system and the operating system
- Identify the people responsible for the old process
- Create a list of all users, errors, system logs, and software interfaces that are replaced
- Provide lists of processes that run on a daily, weekly, or monthly basis
- Document process definitions that are in use and obsolete job definitions
- Identify unsatisfactory scheduling definitions and executions

Scheduling Environment

The team should analyze the impact on the organization's major operational systems. They consider their size, complexity, and their value to the business. The team should be aware of bottlenecks or constraints in the old processes. They should identify all manual schedules or coordination required to maintain the system.

To do this, they should document

- The way administrators manage systems, personnel, and schedules

- Peak activity times and the number of processes that run during these times
- The number of processes that use CRON, DBMS_JOB, and other features and the types of automation used
- Processes that are scheduled using dataset triggers, file arrival, and others

Organizations have developed systems without standard commands and messaging structures. Your administrative staff may not have documented the process dependencies. As you remove applications, or move them into the BPM/BR environment, you will discover these hidden facts. The process of formally defining the communications and sequential requirements is not only a transition task—it is a knowledge management task.

You must develop details for each process. The outcome is to create a procedural outline for the operational system. You need this to validate process outcomes, resolve incidents, or provide systems administration warnings. The result is a process review, built for proactive maintenance activities.

Transition Plan Results

The results of transition planning are

- A list of the conversion team, including a team leader
- Software/hardware configuration map
- Identification of functionality gaps between BPM/BR and the methods being replaced
- Completed security matrix
- Outline of implementation strategy

Migration of Legacy Processes

If the legacy processes are part of the project, then these need to be part of the transition to a new system. In migration, the old schedule information should be moved into business process control. You find old scheduling and process coordination information in legacy practices. These include DBMS_JOBS, **crontab**, programs, and scripts. The new business process is responsible for this coordination. The scheduling definitions are added to BPM/BR scheduling definitions through the BPM monitor.

Your administrators need to tune and adjust the BPM suite using enterprise management tools. When migrating many legacy practices, I recommend that one or two applications be chosen as pilots. By carrying out a pilot, the employees involved in the conversion have the opportunity to become familiar with BPM on a smaller scale.

In the pilot, BPM should monitor a few scheduled or event-driven processes. The pilot should be business processes typical of the organization. It should also simulate typical scheduling complexities, job flow structure, and interactions with other applications. A successful pilot implementation is the foundation for replacing the rest of the site's legacy processes. BPM/BR supports either phased or full conversions, thereby providing the ability to convert one process at a time or the entire enterprise center at once.

Migration of Legacy Processes Results

The results of migration of legacy processes are:

- Process schedule tables.
- Calendars of procedures and events.
- Old system documentation.

TESTING AND VALIDATION

An independent testing team should validate the project's deliverables. They should perform regression testing on a separate test environment. Independent teams provide an unbiased view of the quality of the development efforts. This approach improves the confidence in the system. Before starting application validation, the technical team and the business system users should develop and agree on testing procedures and documentation. Some BPM tools and BRRs can develop queries and use case steps that generate test scenarios.

Testing is simplified when the application's architecture is built with loose coupling. There are fewer dependencies among the parts of the applications. SOA improves stability because each component can be proven to function according to the requirements. In this way, capability is verified in a cumulative way.

Application validations can build confidence in the immediate application while reducing the downstream testing efforts.

Regression testing is a type of testing that attempts to exercise all features of an application. The testing team can develop scripts with regression testing tools such as Rational Robot.

The BRR holds metadata that describe how a system interacts with users and processes. The analysts develop test use cases with queries against the BRR. They also collect validation data sets.

After the team assembles data and scripts, the system should be validated through independent testing and validation. The independent team is responsible for harmonization of the set-up and testing areas. As they conduct the testing, they create deficiency reports and work with the organization to identify corrective measures.

If the project involves new business processes, interfaces, and rules, then the team should do unit, integration, and acceptance testing. Simple changes to business processes or business rules might not need rigorous testing.

Disciplined testing is critical for successful deployment of any complicated system. The separate roles of business process and business rules simplifies some of the complexities of testing. How organizations test their system depends on the project's goals, yet there are common methods of testing. In general, developers test products of their activities during the phases of BPM/BR. Testing the entire system requires coordination.

Table 8.1 describes the types of testing that must be performed in business process, business rules, and business intelligence environments.

Table 8.1 Testing required in different environments.

Type	Description
Process unit testing	Testing of the flows of the business process. Test messaging control.
Business rules unit testing	Test business rules against business cases.
Business intelligence unit testing	Test metrics against the computed benchmarks in the test data set.
Business process and business rules integration testing	Load business processes with data from business cases that exercise rules with expected outcomes.
Business process and interface integration testing	Verify target system receives expected business process inputs and translations are correct
Business intelligence and ETL process testing	Verify that test transactions feed data warehouse schema properly
Acceptance testing	Verify application meets business requirements

Acceptance testing is done by, or in conjunction with, the people for whom the system is being created. These are often the people who use the system when it is put into production.

The team conducts unit and integration tests in the various phases of BPM/BR. Acceptance testing is done as a final check before putting the system into production.

Test Plan

The requirements of the system direct the system testing. A test plan is created in the transition planning phase. This test plan specifies how the system is to be tested and what requirements the system must meet before it is put into production.

The functional and technical specifications outline the exact procedure used to conduct the tests—both at a component level and at an integrated system level. These specifications include

- Type of data to use
- Expected output
- Who is responsible for the test

Test Data Sets

A complete test plan specifies the test data sets. At the unit and the integration levels, your team should use data that follow scenarios that reflect the business process. Where possible, test data sets should come from legacy systems. The scenarios should exercise as many process paths as possible. In addition to real-life data, create data designed to test the system's error handling. You might manually construct or generate this data.

Performance testing needs large volumes of data. The volume of data should match the conditions of the business operations.

Test Plan Results

The test plan includes specifications for

- Exceptions handling
- Transaction performance
- Flow of information
- Transformation of data
- Test data sets, business scenarios, and volume testing

Unit Testing

In unit testing, developers verify their work before integration testing. Each part of the system must be unit tested before the component becomes part of the new application or process. It is useful to develop a unit testing procedure as a part of the technical specifications. In the absence of test procedures, the developer should verify that their part performs according to the specifications.

Integration Testing

Integration testing verifies that new components work together and in the organization's environment. If the system is complex, you should divide the testing into steps. Each step should test a part of the system. For instance, you might verify that transactions move from a file to an interface. A partial test would be to verify that the data can be sent from the file to the interface.

Performance Testing

Performance testing often follows integration testing. Integration testing validates a system's expected operations. Performance testing verifies the adequacy of the system's speed. The testers should test system performance after the system is correctly working.

Another aim of performance testing is to find the bottlenecks in the system. A composite of many factors affects performance. Because of unknown obstructions, tuning a slow process or rule might not improve system performance. Uncovering these bottlenecks shows developers where to improve processing speeds.

In the test plan, the organization should estimate expected and peak volumes. This volume will define the needed performance level.

Stress Testing

The testing team conducts stress testing to decide if the system can handle the expected load. With stress testing, the testers overload the system with data to the point of failure. Stress tests process operationally significant transaction volumes and multiple concurrent connections. This is another effective way to uncover network bottlenecks.

Acceptance Testing

Before moving the system into production, users should validate the system as complying with requirements and specifications. You might do acceptance testing for a part of the system or for an entire system. A typical acceptance strategy specifies the capabilities a system needs to go into production. You should also specify who must *sign off* on the new process.

Parallel Testing

It is important to assure integrity of the organization's production process flow. The testing team tests each process before production activation. This might be part of a phased conversion process rather than converting all processes at once.

Following the conversion process, new business processes should be activated in parallel with the old process methods. In this phase, BPM software simulates the production application's operations.

Testing should schedule processes to run in the test environment rather than production. The production managers can validate that business process software will correctly coordinate or schedule the production processes. This should match production system operation. Final processes validation occurs through examination of records and logs.

Testing Results

The results of testing are

- Activation of processes in test environment mode to simulate processes in production environment in parallel with the old environment
- Adjustment and validation of converted elements
- Review of organization's support staff skills
- Organization's staff is familiar with BPM/BR

PRODUCTION

If the project is a new business process, then the branching and networking of each activity should be balanced with service-level requirements. If you can isolate an activity as a unit, then you can evaluate compliance with SLA constraints. For instance, an activity runs in parallel after a financial application has closed the accounts on a billing period. Other processes might need the updated data to finish.

After completing all previous phases, the organization's business should run with new business processes. At this stage, the organization's IT systems should switch from the old process to the new application.

Production Results

The results of production are

- Activation of converted elements in *production* mode
- On-site support and fine-tuning during the transition phase
- Completion and delivery of operation guide

SUMMARY

Once a process or business rule is in production, there are more considerations. A BPM approach creates loosely coupled applications, and this can change the systems architecture.

In the chapter on IT convergence, I described a strategy for unified scheduling and controlling processes. Unified process control is an important part of BPM. Adopting BPM will need a migration of different needs across scattered systems. Many operational systems are a myriad of processes, data feed loads, and extracts that have become difficult to support. These all feed the IT ecosystem. Many organizations are dependent on a team of technical personnel to monitor and control this complicated environment. A goal of BPM, in the IT convergence phase, is to improve this. The BPM team can add new capabilities and improve service conditions for your users. In this environment, there is a driving need for an integration of the processes that is accessible by both nontechnical managers and systems administrators.

With the system in production, administrators should monitor system activity, check for errors, and change configurations. Monitoring system activity is critical for the long-term success of the system. Routine checks measure long-term performance benchmarks. Such benchmarks help in identifying undesirable changes. If you cannot identify a healthy system's vital signs, you will not know when your system needs attention.

The test environment is the only mature way to verify and refine the system configuration that was set up earlier in the deployment process. Focusing on the transition plan ensures the smoothest possible deployment. By unit testing and system testing thoroughly in the test environment, you will avoid costly errors and satisfy the end users with the results.

CHAPTER NINE: CONCLUSION

Six months have passed and Sumter has now entered the production phase of new processes for maintenance management, customer relations, and BI for inventory management. Equipment managers have shifted from working with reams of printouts and clipboards to focusing on the needs of their customers. The simplicity of the system has rooted out many hidden problems. The IT process team has added all retail stores. Because SAP PM has accurate odometer data, Sumter managers see a clearer snapshot of the age and condition of the rental fleet.

With the new customer relationship process, Sumter negotiated discounts with over 50 of the largest construction firms in their service area. Armed with reports and the new BI tools, managers can evaluate the benefit of each of these contracts—such as, "do these customers lease more equipment for longer periods of time." The new process writes a record when a customer cannot reserve the equipment they need. Retail managers are looking at this data. They have found that verbal contact with the customer was best after they tried to reserve equipment three times. Because of this feature, local stores have improved their sales.

The BI system is yielding many tactical benefits. In one example, a regional manager found a city with several large residential construction projects. It came from an analysis of high lease use rates of the bulldozers normally used in residential construction. Sumter managers were able to move underutilized equipment to the affected stores. This is an example of how BI and business area monitoring produce timely information that can be used for tactical business advantages.

BPM/BR has positioned Sumter's critical rules and processes for change. For instance, managers can add rules that direct store personnel to call customers after their third try to reserve an equipment type. This change can happen without programming. Sumter has discovered through BI and insight gained from the recent changes that the average time from order to delivery is two weeks. Because average transport time is only two days, managers aim to improve the paperwork-intensive process of transporting large orders. Sumter management will target order fulfillment for the next round of BPM/BR improvements. Management believes that a new order process will cut fulfillment to one week, resulting in a revenue increase of $5 million for each year.

Six months into Sumter's first BPM/BR project, the critical metric for the ROI, actual lease rates (ALR) is improving. Each percentage of improvement in the ALR improves profitability by 2-3 percent. The ROI target was to improve the ALR by 1 percent.

The business of equipment leasing has many complex interactions. Profit margins are connected to a combination of business operations, economic demand, and Sumter's ability to tune equipment inventory. There are many equipment types—some targeted for narrow construction needs. Also, construction varies seasonally. Combining business process improvements, business rules and business intelligence yields powerful investigation tools for these dynamic interactions. Improvements can also be quantified.

Finally, the CIO takes a two-week vacation.

DISCUSSION

I have spoken much about the Business Process Management and business rules (BPM/BR) approach. Part of my aim with this book was to show you how to use these techniques to create and maintain your applications. The techniques create solutions with little traditional programming. Using BPM/BR is simple—business rules and business processes meet your critical needs. BPM/BR also manages and maintains the operational system after it is in production. This approach changes the activities of the development team from the traditional engineering process to the business needs of the application it is supporting.

Even though organizations have not discovered them, each has business rules and business processes that are unique. I call these the *cultural* practices. BPM/BR's purpose is to create a composite application for the cultural practices. For instance, a retailer, bank, or telecommunications company might use SAP as its ERP, but it develops its own Web storefront for branding and other competitive activities. The Web application is part of the business process and must interact with the business rules. BPM/BR does this for you.

In the past, a business process was tightly bound to the system that performed the reports and accounting. To change the system, developers must change all computer programs that move data from one system to another.

The BPM/BR easily adapts to new or changing rules and processes because the components of the system are not tightly bound. Web services create the loose binding. With Web services, processes, rules, or system interfaces are published as a specification. Organizations that do this are moving to Business Process Execution Language (BPEL). Processes orchestrate Web services with BPEL.

Business analysts who are able to produce finished business solutions create the solution with the BPM/BR. These *super users* use the BPM/BR design environment to create prototypes to solve a problem. The traditional role of the development team is to carry out requirements, separate from the business experts. This approach brings the business personnel into the development process and the results are efficient. This is what the IT industry calls *self-service* because it provides rapid acknowledgments when it immediately shows the results of adjustments to a business rule.

Like most methods, a team uses the BPM/BR to develop applications in a repetitive, interlocking process. The BPM/BR process is comprehensive because it builds all the parts of today's IT environment in the cycle. It develops by refining business processes, then business rules, then integrations and BI components. What most distinguishes a BPM/BR approach from other cyclical methods is that commercial software packages play a vital role in developing the integration architecture. These packages include the BPM suite, business rules engines, managed query environments, and ERPs.

The BPM/BR team delivers solid IT solutions with a round-trip industrial process. This process draws on the disciplines of methodology, quality, and domain know-how. Figure 9.1 presents the components of what I call a *composite application factory*. Each of the triangles represents a virtual workstation. As they design changes to the composite system, knowledge workers sit at workstations and model business processes, business rules, and BI, then evaluate and publish the results. There is little coding because the designers specifications become the program. Work flows from workstation to workstation through a series of environments. In this environment, methodology, transition quality, and domain know-how allow the activities to be well-coordinated and efficient. Methodology, transition, and domain environments allow the work to be efficient, correct, and productive. The environments of methodology, transition, and domain expertise provide the delivery mechanisms for the work flows.

An important part of the entire deployment project is change management. If changes are needed, they must be processed through the same cycle of planning, development, testing, transition-to-production, and maintenance as the rest of the deployment.

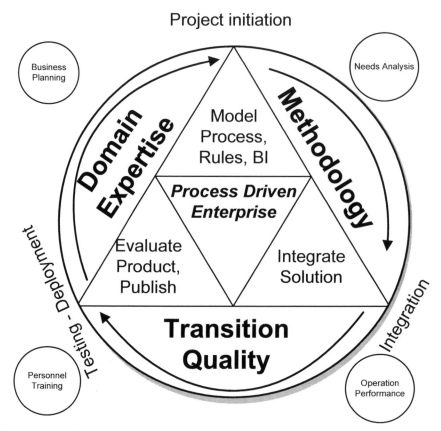

Figure 9.1 BPM/BR is a simplified method of selecting the right software for integrating the components of an EAI environment. COTS software plays a vital role in the architecture.

THE PERFORMANCE GAP BETWEEN TECHNOLOGY AND IT MANAGEMENT

I consider the gap between business objectives and the old methods of information technology to be similar to recent technological changes in the television industry. In the past five years, the changes in the cable and satellite television industry have been dramatic. There is Video on Demand, interactive services, and even integration with Web technology. Yet, look at how long it is has taken the U.S. government and the industry to create digital television standards for broadcast signals. The technological realities—decades old standards, broadcast frequencies, analog infrastructures—have been in competition with the new ways of bringing television to the public.

As with many new technologies, High Definition Television (HDTV) is the subject of a bureaucratic struggle among competing interests. Much of the struggle has been over the gargantuan piece of radio frequency—or bandwidth—occupied by the old standard. Television is broadcast on the airways across a 70-year old radio spectrum. This bandwidth, which might hold more than 100 channels for each analog channel, has the potential to host multitudes of channels for public and commercial communication. Cable and satellite television carriers, however, would prefer to avoid the competition. This unrealized capacity could create a massive, new communication infrastructure for the public's use. The self interests of licensed broadcasters, cable television operators, and others have clashed with the government's objectives in creating fair use for the radio spectrum.

The airway bandwidth occupied by the old TV standards is a metaphor for a business IT system. It has existed for many years and it performs a valuable role—however, the delivery of the capabilities and information is wasteful. It is too expensive and time-consuming. The competing interests and objectives of software companies, business managers, and IT delivery teams have created a business risk for adopting new IT technology. The risk is that proposed or mandated changes in a corporate method climate might unleash a wasteful struggle for funding, personnel, power, and authority. For instance, supporters of aged software systems, tools, and methods (programming in the small) might prefer to avoid the competition. Exposing interfaces and processes to the enterprise as Web services (programming in the large) removes the mystery of how a system works, and that encourages a competitive environment. Because organizations have poorly integrated and fragile software, much of this conflict is affixed to staying in the past. This results in a low ROI. There is also a shortage of properly trained professionals for improving the IT ecosystem. Because operational managers are already busy running the business, they are reluctant to take on the added efforts needed to adopt commercial software that handle BPM and the business rules approach. The legacy system might also be abandoned, or parts of it replaced, by smaller applications and integrations with the new software. Adding a competitive practice—one that can improve the productivity of the business—is similarly difficult.

On a project that managed the communication spectrum for the DoD I learned that the television spectrum occupies an enormous space in our airways. It will be years, if not decades, until it becomes available for modern use (see http://www.ntia.doc.gov/osmhome/allochrt.html).

The potential of improved management practices, including BPM, business rules, and BI software—modern machinery for competing in the economy—is arguably similar to the communication bandwidth occupied by television broadcasters. Both of these potentials are underutilized. Both of these will reap vast rewards for society, and economic efficiencies dictate their use. Just as government and private broadcasters must finally agree on the television bandwidth, the corporation must strive to keep its IT infrastructure integrated, efficient, and competitive. IT must align enterprise IT ecosystems with modern practices in the face of a tangled world of operational, legacy, and ERP systems. Therefore, I refer to the new technology stacks, commercial software, BI tools, integration tools, and hardware as *competitive bandwidth*—an environment that is perfectly formed. The Mandate of Business Process Management and Business Rules

For all enterprises, including governments and nonprofits, there is a basic principle that should be in their IT strategy—business software must efficiently use the competitive bandwidth available to them. To do this, they should lower the cost of inhouse systems whenever they can by replacing them with commercial ERP software products.

For the rest of their operational applications, data warehousing, and integration, they should look to BPM/BR. This means that your programming staff should stop programming *in the small*. The rest of the IT needs of the enterprise should be built with methods that adapt to the changes that are cost effective and efficient through all business cycles.

Remember Mr. Carr's comment that the biggest risk to IT is overspending. If you are not using BPM, then someone in your organization is creating programs in Java, C#, and others that do this. If you are not using business rules software, then someone in your organization is creating programs that do this—or worse yet, they are scattering business rules across a slew of programs.

To expand their use of this competitive bandwidth, organizations should cut out outdated models of problem-solving and create an architecture that is synchronized. By synchronized, I mean that the systems do what the business needs it to do, not what legacy systems developers created it to do. Synchronization is carried out with a method that provides business managers with the information technology they need. In this book, I have suggested that you can deliver this by adapting a strategy that includes a combination of Business Process Management and a business rules approach (BPM/BR). I have described how these new tools improve construction of the application, integration, and BI. The result is a powerful system that saves the organization time and money by allowing it to operate the system with a smaller, more skilled staff and shorter development cycles.

Companies have introduced many different technologies into their IT infrastructure, yet their addition does not always yield all the benefits that they wanted.

BPM/BR modernizes the way today's business information architectures are built. It replaces outmoded ways of developing the IT environment. Organizations have hung competitive technologies from their enterprise IT ecosystem with hardwired retrofit-style methods. These retrofits resulted in a rigid technical architecture. BPM/BR overcomes this by addressing integration, data warehousing, and applications in one step. It avoids retrofitting the environment by creating loosely coupled components whose connections can help new solutions, commercial software, or analytical tools.

The new models suggested by BPM/BR have potentially decreased or ended the need to program many artifacts. It includes

- **Business Process Management (BPM)**—A management technology that models the core processes of the enterprise and isolates them from the systems that are responsible for them
- **Business Rules Approach**—A technique of describing, modeling, and forming engines that interpret the constraints, policies, and basic data needs of the enterprise
- Exposure of the components as Web services to the right organizations in and outside the organization. This enables the composite application—a series of independent systems and capabilities that appear unified to the users and customers

COTS software has modernized many systems, and these also must be integrated.

SUMMARY

When a designer solves a problem domain, he begins by creating an abstract model. For a solution to be worthy, its model must be able to adapt to reasonable changes to the requirements without doing great violence to the core of the assumptions. In computer science, the abstraction provides an accommodation to a programming problem, as expressed in the data structures and code. The levels and degree of abstraction allow the solution to contribute to all the requirements that surround the problem domain. The Business Process Management with Business Rules (BPM/BR) approach is an abstraction of business. Yet, so is computer code. There is a fundamental difference.

The act of listening to a musical composition is an expression of the monoidal nature of consciousness. The composer inscribes (with pen and paper) the notes of the music, musicians perform the music at a recording studio, and its sound becomes output for the listener to enjoy. Each artifact—the paper manuscript, the performance, and the listening experience—is a form of the same item. It is not inconceivable that the listener could come up with a technique for recreating the manuscript by hearing the recorded media—similarly, an ensemble, or performer, could reproduce a performance from such an auditory experience. Paper notations of musical ideas have a *convertible basis* from the data shared across representations.

Business information, including processes, rules, and metrics, is a convertible basis of capabilities in the enterprise. BPEL is a modeling form that reflects a business process. It is a document that reflects a process diagram that depicts a physical process. Methods, like BPM, have their roots in business practices. It is easy to imagine how a business process moves from the business process modeling diagram to the truck delivering inventory or a factory producing products. It is not so easy imagining a huge pile of Java or C# script making the same leap.

The objective of an abstract, monoidal design is to allow core business processes to be transformed seamlessly into applications, interfaces, and business facts. These transformations are created through abstracting business process, rules, and intelligence.

In this book, I have described the important activities of this composite method (BPM/BR), and the important roles of the team members that approach these problems. I have contrasted the BPM/BR with the outdated methodologies by showing how it incorporates new standard practices into developing and maintaining the IT ecosystem. The contrast is the in the abstractions afforded by these methods.

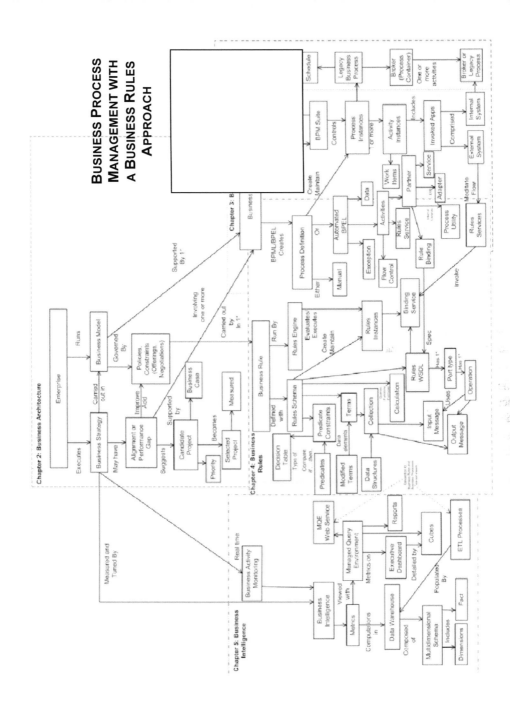

BUSINESS PROCESS MANAGEMENT WITH A BUSINESS RULES APPROACH

Glossary

Activities: An activity is a business process component that performs a specific function. In a business process diagram, activities include the programs that process data, services from applications, and Web services. Flow control is also a type of activity.

Activity Instances: An invoked instance of an activity in a business process, as invoked by the Business Process Management (BPM) suite.

Adapter: An adapter is software that works with BPM suites. Adapters provide prepackaged services for ERPs and transaction standards. Adapters simplify integration.

Alignment/Performance Gap: A discrepancy between a business strategy or model and the services that the systems provide. A BPM/BR project corrects this discrepancy.

Automated BPEL: The part of BPEL that describes software services and utilities.

Binding Service: In WSDL, this refers to the process associating protocol or data format information with an abstract entity like a message, operation, or portType.

BPM Suite: Software that comprehensively designs and manages business processes and monitors their execution.

Business Activity Monitoring: The combination of BPM and Business Intelligence (BI). Business activity monitoring implies real-time data.

Business Case: The business case addresses, at a high level, the business needs that the project seeks to resolve. It includes the reasons for the project, the expected business benefits, the options considered (with reasons for rejecting or carrying forward each option), and the expected costs of the project.

Business Intelligence (BI): An umbrella term for a set of concepts and methods for improving business decision-making by using a fact-based system. BI supports business strategy by creating a tool for measuring and tuning the outcome.

Business Model: The mechanism by which a business intends to generate revenue and profits. For government and nonprofits, it is the mechanism by which the organization intends to carry out its mission.

Business Process: A sequence of activities that carries out a goal and is complete in some way. It is a full orchestration of activities that has an important aim or purpose.

Business Process Management (BPM): The identification, understanding, and management of business processes that link with people and systems in and across organizations

Business Process Extended Language (BPEL): The Business Process Execution Language (BPEL) is a programming language, serialized in XML, that is intended to enable the high-level state transition logic of a process.

Business Process Modeling Notation (BPMN): A standard created by the Object Management Group for graphically describing BPEL. BPMN is done in graphical user interfaces.

Business Rule: The mediator of computer systems or people, such as managers, employees, and salespeople, that decides with information. Example: a policy, a constraint, or a regulatory requirement.

Business Rule (BR) Approach: A design technique for formalizing an enterprise's critical business rules in a language the manager and technologist understand.

Business Rule Repository (BRR): Software and data structures that retain and configure business rules. Metadata in the BRR provides instructions to an instance of a business rule, run by the rules engine.

Business Strategy: A plan or campaign that a business or organization uses to carry out their business model.

Candidate Project: In business architecture, this is a project that might align IT systems with a performance gap or other needs.

Collection: In business rules, this is an array or record set.

Computation: In business rules, this means formulas, selections of data such as the maximum or minimum value, or statistical trends. In this text, transformations are also considered computations.

Cubes: In BI or data warehousing, a cube is the mapping between the data that stores the facts and dimensions and the information that describes prompts and column headings (metadata). The cube is also a user-friendly connection between a manager's point-and-click and the technical query.

Data Structures: In business rules, a data structure is a database table or data source that the rule uses to create records in an operational data store.

Data Warehouse: A set of database tables that hold the dimensions and facts—the MQE—and the processes that populate and manage the data.

Decision Table: In business rules, a decision table is a data-driven collection of predicates (if … then … else), designed to be easily manipulated by business users.

Dimensions: In BI, a holder of descriptive detail, including types, categories, or named entities (customers, orders, and others) from the business ideas.

Enterprise: A business, government, or nonprofit organization that has a mission.

ETL Processes: A type of business process that performs extraction loading and transformation of data into a data warehouse.

Exception: In BPEL, an exception is an unexpected system, process, or data failure.

Exceptions Management: In BPM, a procedure for notification, elevation, and communication of process exceptions.

Executive Dashboard: In BI, a graphical depiction of executive decision metrics.

External System: In BPM, a system that exists outside the enterprises.

Fact: In BI, a numeric attribute that is associated with a dimension. Facts are also called measures. Facts are usually numerical inputs into metrics.

Flow Control: In BPEL, a flow control is an activity that directs other activities in the processes. Examples of flow control include switch statements and while loops.

Input Message: In Rules WSDL, the data that the business rule needs to evaluate a rule.

Internal System: In BPM, a system in the enterprise ecosystem.

Invoked Apps: In BPM, an application that a process needs services from.

Managed Query Environment (MQE): Commercial software that provides tools for building and managing cubes, executive dashboards, and reports.

Manual: In BPMN, a manual process is a process that takes personnel to finish.

Metrics: A system of parameters or ways of quantitative assessment of a business model or process that is to be measured, along with the processes to carry out such measurements. Metrics define what is to be measured. Metrics are usually specialized by the business model or strategy. Metrics assess the present state of business and prescribe a course of action.

Modified Terms: In business rules, specialized types or categories.

MQE Web Service: A Web services interface to the MQE.

Multidimensional Schema: A table layout that is developed from multidimensional analysis is a design that groups data into two basic categories—dimensions and facts. Multidimensional analysis supports the ability to execute a multidimensional query that supports the summarized data across one or more nested, logical groups.

Operation: In WSDL, an operation is the function that you invoke when running the Web service. A WSDL may have many operations.

Operational Data Store: A database designed to integrate data from many sources to simplify operations, analysis, and reporting.

Output Message: In WSDL, the output of a Web services operation.

Partner: The part of BPEL that describes the programs and external services that are used by business processes.

Policies, Constraints (Offerings, Negotiations): The aggregate of the enterprise governance of a business model. Many explicit business rules enforce these.

Port Type: In Web services, defines the exposed operations (similar to a function call in programming languages). Usually there is an input, an output, and a default port type.

Predicate Constraints: A predicate guard.

Predicates: In business rules, a statement of a business rule in an *if ... then ... else* form. Business rules predicates resolve to true or false.

Process and Systems Monitoring: Systems administration in a business process environment.

Process Instances: An instance of a running process that is developed from a process definition.

Process Utility: In the BPM suite, activities use localized services to carry out basic functions such as scheduling, start, and stop.

Rules Engine: In business rules software, the rules engine is the mechanism through which the business rules are run. Rules engines use the metadata, or rules schema, to develop the execution steps.

Rules Instances: An invocation of a business rule, as run by the rules engine.

Rules Schema: The metadata that retains business rules.

Rules Service: The Web services interface to the business rule.

Rules WSDL: An XML format for describing Web services. Rules WSDL is the WSDL for a business rule.

Selected Project: A project deemed worthy of completion due to a solid business case.

Service-Oriented Architecture (SOA): A concept that defines services and is used to support the requirements of software users. The architecture publishes resources to other participants in the network as independent services that the participants can access in a standardized way. Most SOA definitions include Web services.

Work Items: In BPM, work items are activities that are assigned to users in a work flow system.

About Tipping Point Solutions, Inc.

Tom Debevoise is the Chief Technology Officer and cofounder of Tipping point solutions, inc.

From management and economic theories through technical architectures, many ideas offer the *promise* of creating a perfect realm for businesses competing in today's globally networked world. Often, they tout the means to 'close the gap' between management strategies and technical or operational means. Yet the barrier is still demanding. Tipping Point's mission is to deliver this promise through the empowerment and enablement of firms. Empowerment arrises from increasing a firm's maturity in business processes, decisions and business rules. To achieve this, Tipping Point offers a proven catalog of methods, training and consulting services.

Tipping Point's Leadership provide critical practices and approaches for achieving agility across all the enterprise, from the perspective of BPM and the Business Rules Approach. This includes business tactics, changing requirements, enterprise architecture, software, and methodologies. Tipping Point presents its customers with the BPM and decision management approach to the planning, management, and operational actions that are needed to achieve business agility. We help enterprises to create processes that are 'business-agile' – not merely technically agile.

Tipping Point Solutions, Inc. has extensive experience delivering strategic technology services to the commercial market space. Tipping Point solutions empowers organizations to maintain strategic control and governance their processes and decisions. Tipping Point's approach to process improvement solutions is different to the conventional approach for business reengineering. Our approach is to look at an enterprise's business models, promote integrative thinking and deploy tactical, low-cost solutions that never lose sight business-agility needs. Deployment advances at an incremental cadence so one heightens the short-term return on investment while keeping the strategic picture in focus.

As well as training, and mentoring, Tipping Point is a certified channel partner for Knowledge Partners International, creator of the only, vendor neutral comprehensive business rules methodology available.

To read more about Tipping Solutions, Inc. please visit:

www.tipping-point.net

About Knowledge Partners International, LLC.

Knowledge Partners International, LLC (KPI) is recognized as a world leading authority in the field of business rules and decision modeling. Founded in 1996 by Barbara von Halle, KPI was one of the first pioneers to propose and practice the business rules approach.

KPI's book on the business rules approach, Business Rules Applied (2002: Wiley & Sons) has become the standard text for global corporations implementing business rules projects. KPI also published The Business Rule Revolution (2006: Happy About), an anthology of real life experience in implementing business rules solutions by practitioners.

To further aid organizations, in 2004 KPI developed the Rule Maturity Model (KPI RMM) to define, for a given organization's objectives, a cohesive business rules strategy and roadmap for implementation.

KPI has evolved the business rules approach through intense research and development, and even more importantly through practice with some of the world's largest enterprises. These advances include the introduction of a comprehensive business rule mining methodology, and incorporating Business Process Management (BPM) and Service-oriented Architecture (SOA) into the approach.

The tools and techniques developed by KPI may be licensed in a package called KPI STEP, which is fully supported with training and mentoring services by KPI and its global alliance partners. KPI STEP is aligned with the KPI RMM to ensure that organizations evolve their business rules skills and capabilities in line with their business requirements.

KPI STEP enables organizations to significantly reduce cost and risk in BPM, SOA, and other IT development projects while implementing the Business Rules Approach. KPI STEP also provides the means and methods for ongoing management of the business rules and business decisions after completion of the project.

KPI is a privately owned company with offices in New Jersey and North Carolina. We may be contacted at +1 (973) 543-1339 (ext 101), or an the web at www.kpiusa.com

About Intalio, Inc.

Intalio is *The* leading Open Source Business Process Management Suite (BPMS) vendor. Intalio has donated its BPMS server to the Apache foundation, and its BPMN modeler to the Eclipse STP Project. An ongoing effort to promote Open Source continues through its community at bpms.intalio.com. A special website, intalio.org, lists these projects.

Business Process Management is the Service-Oriented Architecture killer application. Intalio helps over 10,000 organizations (as of April 2007) around the world get the highest return on investment from their SOA effort. Highest return is achieved when working with hard, lengthy and intricate processes.

Simplify complex processes. Intalio focuses on giving you the tools for tough business problems, the ones that include thousands of steps if not more. This includes a dependencies tool, run-time versioning, enterprise-class clustering and support for stateful exchange protocols.

With Intalio you design, revise and deploy new business processes without having to write one line of code. One BPMN box replaces 10 lines of BPEL code that in turn replaces 100 lines of J2EE code. Code is bad for agility. Your business flexibility is held back by debugging and IT staff backlog. With graphical development your business people is in control. Intalio's BPMS dramatically reduces your direct development cost and at the same time affords you the needed business agility for real process innovation.

It is Operation System agnostic, supports the latest BPMN, BPEL 2.0, and BPEL4PEOPLE standards. This is essential for interoperability, and necessary for intricate and sophisticated processes. The Designer is based on the Eclipse framework, the Server on Geronimo, and as such are cross-platform.

For special requirements Intalio offers its innovative Demand Driven Development option. This allows the outsourced development of special features. More on this at: http://itredux.com/blog/2006/02/13/ demand-driven-development/.

Founded in July 1999, Intalio is a privately-held, venture-backed company located in Palo Alto, California. For more information on Intalio, please call 650-596-1800 or visit www.intalio.com.

Index

Index

te.org[SM]

The Peer-to-Peer Exchange
for Business Process Management
Professionals

SINESS RULES

◡ like to congratulate Tom
⸝voise on his new publication.

⸝emember, on the road ahead,
BPM will lead the way to renewed and
newly-invented processes. A Business
Rules Approach will ensure old rules
give way to agile ones. The powerful
BPM and Business Rules combination
is only in its first generation.

BPMInstitute.org is pleased to have
Tom Debevoise as a Business Rules
Training Instructor, Business Rules
Symposium Speaker and Frequent
Contributor to the Business Rules
Bulletin – our monthly newsletter
featuring timely articles, research,
white papers, and more.

Visit www.BPMInstitute.org/BR
for the latest information to ensure the
success of your BPM/BR initiatives.

We look forward to serving you.

Best regards,

Gregg V. Rock
Editor & Founder
BPMInstitute.org

BUSINESS RULES
Home Page
www.BPMInstitute.org/BR

TOM DEBEVOISE

BPMInstitute.org's Business Rules
Training Instructor, Business Rules
Symposium Speaker and Business
Rules Bulletin Frequent Contributor

BUSINESS RULES
SYMPOSIUM

The Business Rules Symposium is
the leading event for Business and
IT Professionals seeking an unbiased
source of education, expertise and
guidance on their Business Rules
initiatives.

Visit www.BPMInstitute.org/BR
for dates and locations.

1698549